MIDDLE
SCHOOLED

· · · · · ·

Parenting Tips and Reminders to Keep You Smiling

Andy Mullen

This book is dedicated to my family.
Toni, Drew, Jake and Maggie

Table of Contents

February

March

April

May

June

Introduction
· · · · · ·

Hello Middle School Parents!

They don't mean it. They really don't. Middle school aged children can't help acting like the highly unstable creatures they are. I have lived in the adolescent middle school jungle for 16 years as both a parent and school counselor, recording my observations very much like Jane Goodall did with chimpanzees. My thoughts ended up getting the best of me and found their way into weekly e-mail messages that I have been sending out every Friday to the parents of my students. You could consider this book a "greatest hits" of the weekly messages. *Middle Schooled* is loosely arranged by month. September refers to the start of school, December the holidays, etc. I recommend reading this book at night after a glass of wine, while waiting in the car line, in between games at a tournament or at a concert when your kid is not performing. Reading a little each week or all at once works too. You can also use it as a reference book when a certain topic applies to you and your family. Let's say your child is making up stories and lying to you like crazy. You can totally lose your mind or simply refer to the table of contents, and flip to the message covering lying. Easy! I have tried to cover the most relevant topics for middle school parents and have done so in a way that is both informative and entertaining...

I hope you'll agree!!!

Andy

September

· · · · · ·

Hello Middle School Parents!

It was not urgent at the time. There were always so many other things to do. We put it off, leaving it languishing on the back burner. Out of sight out of mind. Every once in a while, we would discuss it, but we never implemented a plan of action. What could another day, week, month or year matter? There is always tomorrow. Time slowly slipped by, as it has a way of doing, until it was too late.

This morning at 6:30 my daughter came down the stairs, pointing her finger at her two older brothers. "I had to take a cold shower because of you two," she bellowed, as they ate their beautiful whole wheat pita pockets delicately stuffed with a fire roasted onion and red pepper omelet kissed with a Mexican blend of cheese, hand made by their loving father… but I digress. The indiscretion was, that due to their selfishly long showers, there was no hot water left for the rest of us. I heard this news and knew better. Time, fueled by procrastination, had won the race. I grabbed a flashlight which was out of batteries, picked up a head lamp that was not charged, finally settling on a small keychain dinosaur light that roared when I turned it on (obviously a frivolous purchase by an unidentified grandmother). Horrible words tumbled from my mouth with regrettable ease as I ran down to the basement to investigate, even though I knew what I would find. Within seconds, my socked feet were marinating in an energetic river of tepid water carrying the remains of old Nerf gun "bullets" my kids played with years ago. The water heater had rolled a 7. Why did I wait so long to get a new one?? I just had the water heater installed a few years ago... 14 years ago to be exact, when my oldest son was 2 my wife reminded me. The routine of life and work had succeeded in accelerating time to a dangerous speed. The water heater and Nerf gun debris gave me pause, and a fresh view of the passage of time.

In my wet socks and boxer shorts, dinosaur light in hand, I thought back to what a father said to me at the high school graduation 3 years ago as he was watching his amazing and accomplished daughter graduate. With tears in his eyes, he said, "I missed it. I missed all of it." He was talking about his child and not spending enough time with her. He had waited too long...

Do it now! Whatever is on your bucket list as a parent and a family, the time is now. Spend time with your children while you can. This window of time is so small, roughly the average life of a water heater. Go to the game. Take that walk. Build that chair. Prioritize and do the stuff you want to do and stop procrastinating! Move these important family experiences to the front burner. Make a plan of action and do it!

This weekend my son and I are going to build a mahogany recycling bin with inlayed lettering. I think 10 coats of a marine spar varnish might be nice!

I hope you have a great weekend!

Andy

• • • • • •

Hello Middle School Parents!

I don't know about you, but my children have been so eager for the start of school! You can only sleep in, spend time with friends and family and enjoy life to the fullest for so long. It gets old. The kids keep saying things like, "School is awesome! I am so excited to open the gift of education each and every day," "The birds sound so pretty at 5:00 in the morning" and "I love homework more than my Rainbow Flip Flops and Uggs." Seeing the bus lights coming down the road on a foggy morning produces a giddy euphoria in the children akin to past reported sightings of Rudolph the Red Nosed Reindeer...

The start of school can be crazy and stressful for families. Below are a few tips and reminders that might help to make the transition back to school a little easier:

- Reestablish the daily routine: Bed time, dinner time, wake up time. These all need to be slowly brought back from the summer time "do what you want when you want" routine.

- The homework is going to start pouring in. Make sure they have a quiet place to do their work and that they are managing their time properly. Encourage them to put their phone in a different room while they are working.

- Removing technology from your child one hour before you actually want them to be asleep can be extremely helpful.

- Make sure they have whatever school supplies are needed. My family went to Staples Sunday night before school started. I was able to wrestle the last pack of mechanical pencils from an elderly woman, so it all ended well. In the future, we may choose to make these purchases in advance...

- Talk to your kids. Even though they may not answer in complete sentences or even make eye contact, don't give up! The kids need to know you are interested in their school day.

- Be optimistic about the start of school. We all know it's tough but stay positive in a realistic way. Remind them about the things they enjoy about school. Friends, nice teachers, tater tots, the smell of the hallways on humid days. (After 16 years I finally figured it out. The smell when the kids come in from recess period is room temperature Italian deli meats mixed with red onion, Axe Body Spray and unkempt recycling bins.)

- Plan healthy dinners ahead of time. If you can make some dinners over the weekend and freeze them, even better. I am happy to share some of my recipes upon request.

- If your middle schooler is annoying you, consider buying them #3 pencils (you may need to mail order these from Canada) and folders with puppies on them.

Middle school is like space travel in many ways. If your child's heat tiles fall off upon reentry to school, please ask for help!

I hope you have a wonderful long weekend!

Andy

• • • • • •

Lying

Hello Middle School Parents!

The middle school years can be filled with tremendous accomplishments, growth and maturity. As parents, you can sit back and watch your child steadily evolve into the amazing and confident young person you know that they are. This parenting stuff is easier than growing a Chia Pet... (Insert sound of a needle scratching across a record album.) But wait! You just realized your child has been lying to you for two weeks! Instead of attending track practice, they have been enjoying Iced Espresso Classics at Starbucks and perusing the aisles of Five Below looking for fake plastic vomit and other must have items. What are you going to do!!!! Keep reading, it is all going to be OK!

Believe it or not, lying is part of growing up. While there are many families that don't have issues with their children not telling the truth, many do. Yes, it is wrong, but experimenting with this new-found power is normal. When you think about it, it is amazing. With a few carefully twisted words your child can:

- Avoid negative consequences. (Tell my parents I did my homework and I am still going to the dance. Sweet!)
- Establish their identity with their peers (Forging my parents signature on the Sex Education Unit packet and telling my buddies. I am a loose cannon, a rebel of unparalleled proportions.)
- Prove they are different from their parents or that they feel the rules are too strict (Dress too short. Is that right mom? I will leave the house in sweat pants and pack the mini skirt in my gym bag. Change in the bathroom and I am back in the game!)
- Get some needed attention.
- Avoid hurting someone's feelings (You look nice in that dress Aunt Frumpy... We both know your aunt did look a little big boned in that dress but why make her feel bad? Perhaps this kind of lie you let go? Pick and choose your battles.)

Here are some suggestions that might be helpful in dealing with this problem-solving strategy that can quickly become a bad habit:

- Stay calm! When you catch your child in a lie, don't react. Send them to their room and cool down. Talk to your spouse or other trusted person and come up with a game plan.

- Remember that they are not lying to hurt you. There is probably something going on and they don't know how to deal with it. Yes, they lied and you are mad, but why did they do it? What is the underlying problem they were trying to solve? Ask them!
- Don't start lecturing. They don't listen. Stick to the facts and keep it simple. "I saw you jump out of the window, fall into the recycling bins and run down the road. I know you left the house."
- Have consequences that you can and will follow through with. Keep the emotion out of it.
- Focus on why they felt the need to lie and discuss other options that might have helped solve the problem in a more effective way.
- Do not engage in arguing. This normally does not help.
- Be a good role model. If you tell lies, your kids will too.
- When they are honest, make a big deal about it. When they mess up, keep your cool. "Thank you for telling me you scratched our new BMW with your hockey stick. Your father and I appreciate your honesty..."

It is our job as parents to help our kids deal with life and guide them through this confusing time. Seriously, it is. Would I lie to you?

I hope you have a great weekend!

Andy

• • • • • •

Hello Middle School Parents!

It caught us all by surprise. The change implemented was unannounced and unanticipated, leaving my family reeling. My wife, in an unprecedented move, made the executive decision to change from Scott's to a premium brand. The quilted, plush thickness, in stark contrast to our normal, less hardy product, thrust us deep into a perplexing quandary. How much do we use in order to attain the desired results while simultaneously avoiding a myriad of undesirable "incidents?" (A similar thing happened when we switched to a less frothy dish soap, but that story is for another time...) This modern-day dilemma, which we have come to terms with, is in many ways, like the decisions we must make every day as parents.

The questions of how much, how many and how often is at the forefront of our challenge as parents. Moderation and adaptability may be the key:

- Set reasonable goals and expectations before the school year starts. Monitor the progress once a week. Resist the urge to check it on-line every day. (If you are addicted to checking your kid's grades call 1-800-helicopter for help.)
- Talk to your children every day. The quality of the responses (for boys more often) are so poor that it is easy to want to stop asking the questions. Just the other day, a good friend of mine was up late at night worrying about his lack of communication

with his 11th grade daughter who is an amazing, responsible young lady. The next morning, he blurted out to her while she was eating breakfast, "I love you. Please don't do drugs. Call me anytime you need a ride home and please don't get pregnant, it will really mess things up for you." He told me that, admittedly, his delivery was not all that smooth, and she did look at him like he was crazy, but she "needed to hear me say those words." I think he did the right thing!

- Does your child seem happy? Are they basically doing what you expect from them? Let them do their thing. Don't look for a problem if there is not one. If you look hard enough you will find a problem that your searching helped to create.

- I am hearing more and more students express their annoyance with being "treated like a kid." Take notice of the gradual maturation of your child and adjust your behavior toward them accordingly.

We recently got a new batch of chickens. The rule of thumb is to hold them and interact with them when they are young. Being consistent with this will make the chicks friendlier toward you and more likely to let you pick them up and handle them when they are grown. The same thing is true with your kids. Hug them every day! Tell them you love them. It can be harder as they continue to grow and push you away, but once you stop, it is hard to start it back up again.

I hope you have a wonderful weekend!

Andy

· · · · · ·

Hello Middle School Parents!

OK, here's the situation. My parents went away on a
week's vacation and they left the keys to the brand-new
Porsche. Would they mind? Umm, well, of course not...
(How old are you? Do you know this song??)

Here is what really happened. A few weeks ago, my wife
and I along with 2 of our 3 children went away for the
weekend, leaving our 12th grader at home alone. We left
the keys to the 4-year-old Chevy and, well, nothing happened. No car was taken, no party was held, no live band
was playing Nirvana in our backyard. Something, however, did happen that made me thankful. Upon our return, we asked him if he missed us. He replied, "Well, not
really. I never realized how little I actually see you
guys. The only time I missed you was at dinner."

Ah, yes! The family dinner! We have placed family dinners very high on our list of priorities over the
years. Hearing my son indirectly credit our time together
at dinner as our time to talk and be together made me
happy. Time flies by, and before you know it, they are
driving, taking SATs, looking at colleges, writing essays,
going to clubs and sports at high school, and doing a lot of
other normal older kid activities. The result of this "growing up" is they are spending less time at home, as they
should be. Family dinners are like starting a retirement
account or planting a tree; you need to start now for it to
grow and take root. These roots have provided an anchor
for us and our son and has helped us weather the crazy

storm of growing up. (That was just an analogy fest. Nice!)

Here are some other things to keep in mind about family dinners:

- Family dinners will help you stay involved in the lives of your children.
- Slowing down, listening and spending time with your kids is more important than any practice or lesson they might have.
- Dinners don't have to be fancy. The point, is you are all together.
- Don't hammer your kids with questions. That makes you annoying. Talk and laugh together. Keep it light.
- Don't lecture! That makes you annoying again!!
- No technology at the table. Be a good role model.
- Kids who eat family dinners are less likely to do drugs, drink or smoke (not only at dinner but all the time!!)
- Rituals and routines are very calming for children.
- The more family dinners a week the better.
- Have your kids help prepare and clean up dinner!
- Be present. Listen to what your kids are saying even if you don't really follow it.
- I know you are tired but talk about your day with your children.
- Family dinners will help you to monitor your child's mood and basically stay on top of what they are doing.

I hope you have a wonderful weekend!

Andy

· · · · · ·

Hello Middle School Parents!

You still have time! I am sure of it. (Insert Yoda's voice) I have seen it to be so...

Yesterday on our 5th grade field trip to a local farm, I was reminded of and learned a lot of things that I thought were amazing! The first thing I learned was that watching pigs race around a tiny track is awesome! My love for pigs runs deep; bacon, pork chops and ham make me happy, but watching those festively plump porkers running was inspiring. If they can do it, so can I.

Here is what I was reminded of: Your 5th graders are very much still little kids. Is the "middle school monster," armed with the power to enrage, frustrate, and disobey somewhere nearby? Perhaps. But right now, you still have time to enjoy this innocent, and relatively simple stage of your child's life. I recently saw an ad in a magazine that read, "Take your time, or someone else will." While the advertiser was encouraging consumption of an adult beverage while fly fishing (which sounds fun too), I thought of this as a reminder to slow down and enjoy this time with your children. Time, time, time. This is the time to enjoy your children for the goofy, happy, playful little people they are. They still want you to jump on the trampoline with them, fall asleep on your lap, play games with you and ask you to brush their hair. They still like you and want to spend time with you, so don't miss out! Say yes to the football catch. Say yes to building a fort out of a box. Say yes to building a dam in the creek. Say yes to baking cookies. Do it now!! All the other obligations of life will still be waiting for you. Spend this time with your

14

child because before you know it, they will be all grown up and off to the pig races!

I hope you have a wonderful weekend!

Andy

October

. . . . . .

Flexibility

Hello Middle School Parents!

Being a parent requires a lot of flexibility as well as thinking outside of your comfort zone. If your children are exactly like you or your spouse in every way, then figuring out what activities you should encourage is very easy. You played soccer, your kids will play soccer. Easy. Let's take soccer for example. You know the rules. You know how it is done. You can practice with them, support them, and honestly you enjoy it too. Playing soccer is "in your wheelhouse" as they say. Supporting your child in this area takes very little thought on your part. You sign your kid up for soccer, and you eagerly await discussing his varsity prospects as well as where he will play in college. You later discover that for the past two weeks he routinely kicks the ball into the creek near the fields and ends up building a dam or pulls an old bicycle out of the water and

16

tries to put the chain back on for the remainder of practice...hmm, you never did that.

Over the course of the year, you provide copious amounts of encouragement, redirection, admonishment, and empathy and everything points to the same conclusion: Your child does not like soccer! As a matter of fact, you realize he does not like sports at all! You give away the $149 FIFA approved soccer ball, the Nike Elite socks ($15, seriously?? And who came up with having a right and left sock?) and back to the drawing board. Here is where the rubber meets the road. What do you do? You and your wife played sports and your child does not want to. Where to go from here:

- Stay calm. There are millions of successful, happy, and amazing people who did not play sports. I am pretty sure Bill Gates was not getting blisters on his hands from hanging on the rim too much.
- Take inventory of your own feelings. Many moms and dads have dreams of seeing their child hit the home run or score the game winning touchdown. Learning to love and appreciate your child for their own unique set of gifts and talents is very important.
- At the high school I have seen many students give up sports (both voluntarily and involuntarily) and with the proper encouragement and direction, it can be a blessing. One student got hurt and ended up joining the chess team and loving it. Another student finally "had the courage" to quit field hockey and started volunteering every day after school. She wrote her college essay about it. She has never been happier.

17

- To play sports at a higher level often requires "specializing" and can create a one-dimensional person. Sure, they can "sting the net," but if they don't know how to change a tire, make a cheddar omelet or do their laundry, life later on might be difficult. Always encourage your child not to put all of their eggs in one basket. Save some for the omelet. Make time to nurture some interests and talents that are not connected to their sport. In the event that they leave their sport, they won't be starting from scratch.
- Figure out what your child enjoys and what their strengths are. What activities might take advantage of their skill set? Fishing, cooking, sewing, volunteering, building things-the list is endless. Think about your child and be creative in your suggestions. Especially in middle school, this is where you need to throw enough stuff against the wall and see what sticks. Most attempts will fail, and you must not give up! Children need to find what they are good at. It helps to build their self-esteem and identity. Somebody might use that guitar, tennis racket or karate uniform that are now in the basement. Maybe you can re-gift it to your spouse for your anniversary...or maybe not.
- Take an interest in what they are doing. Learn something new with your child. Take a woodworking class together or take out a book on birding or orienteering. Whatever might be fun, do it. Learn about their interests so you can support them in some way.
- They need to stay physically active, even if they are not playing a sport. (Yoga, hiking, walking the dog etc.) There is something they will enjoy. Physical activity is helpful for their mood and self-esteem.

It might be good for you too! You have been a little grumpy lately.

- Gaining praise for athletic accomplishments is naturally built into our society, but it is harder to come by for the non-sport activities. Be proud of his performance in the musical, his poetry reading, or the garden she helped you build. Make sure he knows how proud you are of him. Let her hear you talking about her accomplishments to your friends and family.

As Elastigirl from the Incredibles said, "I think you need to be a bit more... flexible."

I hope you have a great weekend!

Andy

· · · · · ·

Hello Middle School Parents!

Years back, I had the privilege of being the counselor for a student named Lucy. At our high school she worked extremely hard and earned grades that were not in line with the amount of time she spent studying. She was frustrated but never stopped trying and graduated with hard earned Bs and maybe a few Cs. After her freshman year in college, Lucy called me to tell me that she was getting As at Penn State! She explained that she had finally figured out how to study. Through trial and error, Lucy discovered that she was an auditory learner. She could study note cards all night and the material would not sink in. Instead, Lucy started to record her own voice reading her class notes and making podcasts that she would listen to when she exercised. Through exploration and heightened self-awareness, Lucy had figured out how her brain works and in turn, how to study.

Most middle school students do not know how to study. The reason for this is either they have never had to study, and/or they don't know how they learn. If you stop and think about your child, you most likely know the answer. Can you give three verbal commands (like sit, stay and roll over) and they can remember and accomplish the tasks, or do they have more success if you write down the tasks on a piece of paper? If their coach explains a new drill or play, do they get it right away or do they need to run through it a few times? Think about your child and look for patterns of success. What are they really good at and why? To be good at things you have to learn something first. How did they do it? When you have the answer, apply it to school and studying. Below are some creative study strategies that have worked for my students over the years. Maybe some will work for your child:

- Teach your stuffed animals! Acting as the teacher and talking it out can be a fantastic way to learn. You might be surprised how interested in The American Revolution that old bulldog stuffed animal might be while the stuffed tree frog may prefer science. If the animals respond to your questions, please see your doctor.
- Make a poster of the material you need to learn. If you are a visual learner, during the test, you might be able to picture the poster in your mind and in turn recall the material.
- Watch a documentary, Ted Talks or Kahn Academy on the topic you are learning. If I recall, History of the World Part I (Mel Brooks) should take care of

the entire social studies curriculum through 12th grade.
- Make a podcast like Lucy did! This again, is great for the auditory learner.
- Use a white board and write it out. The actual act of standing up and physically writing can be helpful for the kids who have trouble sitting still.
- Use sidewalk chalk to draw a picture of the map, chart or whatever you need to learn on the driveway.
- Study while doing something fun. Verbally review the material with someone else while shooting baskets or cleaning out the recycling bins.
- Study with a responsible friend and talk it out.
- Take a permanent marker and write out your vocabulary words on the siding of your parents' house. Extension ladders help for the hard to reach places. Step back and admire your work from street level while reading the words aloud to your neighbor's cat.

I hope you have a wonderful weekend!

Andy

• • • • • •

Kids are like dogs

Hello Middle School Parents!

We tried to raise him right, we really did. From the beginning, my wife and I showered him with unconditional love, providing clear rules and expectations for behavior. Never in need of material items and having access to only the best of everything life can offer. He has had every opportunity to succeed. We were fully vested in meeting our responsibilities as parents and doing the best job we could. Then we realized what he had been doing. To our dismay and frustration, we discovered his actions were upsetting the neighbors and most importantly, his choices were putting his life at risk. Our dog had been jumping the fence and enjoying the freedom of gallivanting around our neighborhood, chasing animals and living the good life of a free dog. He thinks the world is his toilet. Nice.

I had just poured a cup of coffee at 5:00 a.m. today and realized the dog was gone. I ran outside in my pajama pants and Crocks (which you can threaten to wear out in public if your kids annoy you) in hot pursuit of my reckless animal. After 20 minutes of walking through the backyards of the neighbors with a high-powered flashlight (that was fully charged and operational!) I found the dog. The anger was coursing through my veins as I held the collar of my 100-pound Blood Hound/Sheppard mix while standing in my neighbor's hydrangea bushes, dreaming of coffee. I wanted to yell at him, to give him a quick smack, to let my emotions take over and then I paused. If I give in to the dark side, my dog will never come back when I call him. He is two years old, in dog years that is 14. Then it hit me. I was dealing with an adolescent dog! (His acne is nonexistent, his teeth are straight, and I like him, so I guess I didn't notice.) Perhaps I should treat my dog like a middle schooler that makes poor choices? Would that work? Let's take a quick look at how dogs and middle schoolers are similar and we can decide together:

- Dogs and middle schoolers both smell when wet.
- It is necessary to repeat commands numerous times to get a response (Sit / Do your homework).

- They both make the house a mess (dogs shed hair / kids shed dirty clothes).
- Both can be very noisy (barking / complaining).
- Both can be stubborn and head strong (Have to pull on the leash to get them to move / bother you incessantly to opt out of state testing).
- They respond well to positive reinforcement (dog treats / money).
- One can experience great difficulty in keeping them in the yard / house when their hormones are in overdrive.
- Dogs and middle schoolers can both benefit from structure with consistent and predictable consequences for their actions. (We are installing an electric fence with shock collars. I wonder if this would work for the kids as well?)

I hope you have a wonderful weekend!

Andy

• • • • • •

Decision making

Hello Middle School Parents!

Have you ever thrown a mattress out of a second-floor window? The way it laboriously flaps in the wind as it plummets to the ground is mesmerizing. It almost looks like it is trying to fly, but most of us know that it can't. This perceived valiant and futile effort of the mistreated mattress is both sad and inspiring all at the same time. More importantly, making this decision to kick the mattress from the nest was extremely easy and made a lot of sense when I was with my middle school friends. Ryan and Sean were twins with a notoriously creative flare for finding unique opportunities for fun. Taking advantage of these opportunities was much easier when coupled with a low to non-existent ability to project future outcomes, consequences and the potential negative impact our actions could have on others. The middle school mind is locked in the here and now, relishing immediate gratification and peer acceptance. Let's take a closer look at the impact friends can have:

- Adolescents in groups (or hormone clusters) can make rash and impulsive decisions. To see some in their natural habitat, go to the local strip mall after school. It is sort of like going to the zoo, but different.
- Kids will say and do things when with their friends that they would never do when by themselves. (sleep over + social media = bad choices)
- Adolescents are more likely to commit delinquent acts when with their peers.
- Risk taking adolescents gravitate toward one another. They are drawn to each other like tornadoes to trailer parks or grandmothers to infomercials. You get the idea.
- Adolescents are happiest when interacting and spending time with their peers.
- Adolescents are very, very concerned and motivated by what their friends think of them. If they can say or do something that in their estimations will advance them socially and/or display some sort of social power, their actions will be driven by this rather than tempered by what they know is right.
- Let me boil this down to the obvious: When your kid is with their friends, you need to keep an eye on them (unless you want your mattress to end up on

the sidewalk). Don't assume because your child has always been amazing, that they are incapable of making poor, peer influenced decisions.

- Lastly, if they do make a "bad choice," it does not mean they are a "bad kid." It means they are under the influence of adolescence and just need to sleep it off (may take 6 years) and grow up. The mattress on the sidewalk might be a good place to rest.

I hope you have a great weekend!

Andy

• • • • • •

Have fun

Hello Middle School Parents!

I think everyone should own a Gorilla suit. You really never know when you will need it. It is even better to have two. One gorilla walking around can be strange. People may think you are weird. If there are two gorillas however, people will start handing you their baby to get a photo, buying you free food and drinks and basically treating you like the novel, interesting, fun imitation primate that you are. Not sure why this is, but I have tried it, and I know it to be true. Why am I telling you about gorilla suits? Well, it fits into having fun with your middle schooler. I will admit, dressing up like a gorilla with your kid and walking around town may not be for everyone. Putting on the suits for the pizza guy, or maybe to skype an elderly aunt, might be more palatable. The point is, having fun with your kids, especially middle schoolers, can take some creativity! Below are a few ideas for how you and your family can have fun this fall:

- Make your kids rake up all the leaves in the yard. Jump in this pile of leaves with your children. Don't worry about errant dog poop, ticks or other unwanted yard debris. You will all have fun. Even better, dress up in your new gorilla suits, hide in the pile and invite your elementary school aged neighbors over to play. It will be a lasting memory.

- Go for a walk or a hike in a local park. Point out the fall foliage and beauty that is all around you. Perhaps this is another good time for your gorilla suits. If you see park rangers, run away or climb a tree.

- Play bobbing for apples. This is fun for the whole family. Try rubbing lard on the apples rendering them virtually impossible for your kids to get. Please check with your child's orthodontist before allowing them to play. Braces can get stuck in the wooden barrel making it difficult to breath.

- Go for a picnic. Prepare warm food and bring it in a thermos. Bring some warm beverages for the adults as well.

- Create a scavenger hunt! Take the time to make up a cool list of items to find and invite some friends over. While the kids are running around, you can relax with your friends. Some good items for the list are leaves, pine cones, or clean recycling bins.

- Play football. Show your kids you still have what it takes. Get some friends and family together and play a game of rough touch football. You may be slower, older, more fragile and have less energy than you did years ago but you can still run a (one) crisp post pattern. I think there is a country song about playing football when you are older: "I ain't as good as I once was, but I am as good once as I ever was."

26

- Make a scarecrow. Clean out a closet or two, get some old clothes and stuff them with straw, etc. Then, put the gorilla suit on the scarecrow and put it in a tree at a busy intersection. Sit in lawn chairs and watch the chaos that follows.
- Lastly, I highly recommend burning stuff. Light the outdoor fire pit. The kids love it. (They tell me parents are less annoying by firelight.) Don't wear the gorilla suits for this. I think the fur is flammable.

I hope you have a wonderful fall weekend!

Andy

• • • • • •

Friend groups

Hello Middle School Parents!

First there was Chris. I met him in 3rd grade and we remained best friends until 5th grade when he hit me with his ceramic dinosaur on the bus ride home. My best friend in 6th grade was Manoj. The best thing about our friendship was eating his mom's amazing Indian food which I did often. I think there was something about a hungry, chubby, red haired boy scarfing down her food with indebted gratitude that kept her cooking for me. Manoj moved to Pittsburg and I resumed eating my Hungry Man Meals. (The cherry pie part was actually pretty good.) Last was Tom. We were buddies and enjoyed collecting comic books and playing Dungeons and Dragons (please don't judge). Then I joined the Middle school football team, instantly became cool, in my eyes anyway, and stopped talking to him. Nice.

The point is, friendships in middle school are fluid! More than half of all middle school friendships don't last a full year. This change is often accompanied by pain, tears, fear and sadness and it is all part of growing up. Watching your child distance themselves from old friends can be scary. It can get really awkward when you are friends with the parents as well. They may also be trying to make new friends with kids you don't know, and this is something they have never had to do before.

Let's take a closer look at why friends are important, what can go wrong and what you can do as parents to help your child:

- Middle schoolers crave acceptance by their peers.
- Friends can be great to talk to about their worries and problems.
- Friends can help give them another point of view.
- Friends share common interests.
- Friends give them a sense that they have someone on their side and that they are not alone.
- Being with friends can be lots of fun.

What could possibly go wrong? Let's take a closer look:

- When interests change, so do friends.
- Friends can exclude each other. Ditching them at the mall or a game, not including them in the inside jokes or group chats.
- Friends can tease each other beyond what is fun and appropriate.
- Attempts to move higher up on the social ladder often requires dumping your old friends.

- There is a desire for power and control over others that helps fuel some of the most egregious behaviors.
- Middle school friendships are highly unstable, to say the least.

How are they being treated by their friends? Is there a consistent record of behavior that is unacceptable? It might be time to move on. What can you do if you are sensing your child may need to make some new friends:

- Remind your child what real friends are like. Words such as trustworthy, respectful, kind, good listener and supportive may come to mind.
- Encourage participation in new activities to meet new people.
- Support and listen to your child. Remind them that friendships don't always last and that is OK.
- Recommend they make arrangements ahead of time to sit with new people at lunch.
- Have them brainstorm a list of kids that they might like to get to know better and how they might go about doing that.
- Remind your child to be confident and smile. They can do it!

I hope you have a wonderful weekend with your friends!

Andy

· · · · · ·

Hello Middle School Parents!

Do you ever have difficulty understanding how your child is feeling? Words from teenagers can be misleading and confusing to adults. Often one word answers don't give us much insight! If you want to know what is going on with your adolescent, take notice of their body language.

Here are some tips and reminders that might help:

- There are often inconsistencies in what the kids are saying and their body language. Your child is probably unware of the mixed messages they are sending.
- Kids can be clueless of how rude their body language can be. Point it out to them. Explain it so they understand.
- Not all non-verbal communication is rude. If you slow down and take notice of your child, you will see what their body language is telling you-sad, happy, angry, frustrated. They are truly an open book if you know how to read them.
- Acknowledge their feelings when you notice them. They want to know that you care and that you are paying attention.

Below is a quick reference guide to understanding your child and their body language. Feel free to print this out, laminate it and keep it handy. It is sort of like a pocket dictionary for understanding a new language, but slightly different:

- Eye rolling: They think you are stupid.
- Sighing: They think what you are saying is stupid.

- Poor body posture / slouching: They are bored with you because you are boring.
- Crossing their arms: They are angry at you because you are mean and stupid.
- Not making eye contact: They are not interested in you or what you are saying. They want to be playing video games.
- Turning their body so they are not facing you: You know even less than they previously thought. Not interested.
- Raising their middle finger: I am not sure on this one, but I think it means they think you are number 1 in their book!

hope you have a wonderful weekend!

Did you just roll your eyes at me??

Andy

November

· · · · · ·

Hello Middle School Parents!

I have a great idea!! Let's have a heated discussion about politics. Seems to be the "in thing" these days. I feel it's highly appropriate for me (your kid's middle school counselor) to bestow my opinionated views on such topics. Always seems to work well in mixed company, late in the evening at dinner parties…hmmm, for some reason I am starting to second guess this idea. I am having flash backs to the times my son exceeded the recommended limits on his diaper or the time I was aggressively scrubbing and polishing my recycling bin and it cracked… Change gears.

Let's talk about adolescent development and how it can impact their views and thoughts about politics. The more you know, the better equipped you will be to help your child navigate and understand this important topic:

- Adolescent's thoughts on politics become more abstract as they get older.
- They start to think more independently.
- Thoughts are more conceptual and less simplistic. (Why do we have laws? A younger child may say something like "So people don't just steal my dad's recycling bins." An older child might respond by saying "Laws keep us all safe and are general guidelines for everyone to follow.")
- Younger children are more inclined to understand having one ruler (like the kings and queens that are in so many kid's movies) instead of a democratic system. Older adolescents, with more empathy appreciate the benefits of a democracy.
- Older adolescents will start to form their own opinions and attitudes. They will start to question ideas and require more information that they are now able to process.
- They start to question the values and beliefs of their parents. (Have you seen this yet? You are in for a treat.)
- They are eager to establish their own ideas and thoughts now that they have the cognitive ability to do so.
- Teens' political thoughts seem to be influenced by the political environment in which they've grown up. (The same holds true for music. The music you love as an adolescent is normally the most meaningful. That is why your wedding song was "Walk this Way" by Run DMC or was it "Here I Go Again" by Whitesnake?)
- Encourage your child to be a good listener and to keep an open mind to ideas that may be different from their own.

- Ask their opinion and model appropriate behavior when having a discussion.
- Acknowledge their new ability to form their own ideas while emphasizing the importance of listening to the ideas of others.
- Enlist the help of other trusted adults in their lives to have these discussions with your child as well. Your kid probably won't listen to you anyway...

I hope you have a wonderful weekend!

Andy

• • • • • •

Hello Middle School Parents!

Is your family normal? Do you ever take pause while in the shower or maybe while making lunches and wonder if you are "doing it right" as a family? If people only knew what went on. It is the unspoken, the mysterious curtain, the wall that we all keep fortified, concealed and protected. The fear of being exposed as a family that might be considered strange, unconventional or out of control, can be paralyzing. But what really is normal? Is being normal a good thing?

Many of the most seemingly normal people I have known are boring and uninteresting. The exhaustive amount of energy and time that must be spent to keep up the image of a happy normal family may leave little room for the creative, exciting and fun. I have some news for you; you are all normal because there is no normal. Over the past 16 years as a counselor, I have come to the conclusion that the only consistent theme in families is the fact that they are all unique and special in their own way.

The real question should be is your family happy. Not all the time, that would be weird, but most of the time. If you answer yes, then breathe a sigh of relief. If you are not, that is reason to take a closer look at the possible causes of unhappiness and formulate a plan of change. Counselors are very good at helping with this.

Below is a well-regarded and heavily studied "Test of Familial Normality" (TFN) that I just made up, which can help reveal if you are on track. If you can find at least 3 of the very normal and common items below that apply to your family, you pass the test:

- Someone is normally yelling in the morning before school.
- Your children fight with each other.
- Your spouse is very annoying some of the time.
- Your laundry room is a total mess.
- You have no idea what to have for dinner.
- Your child does not do all of their homework.
- Your gutters leak.
- You don't know the name of the neighbor that lives behind your house.
- Finding time to think is difficult.
- You have secret fears that your wife will turn out like her mother.
- Your dog eats food off the counter.
- Your pets and kids ruin the sofa.
- You wonder why there is not better parking at Wegman's.
- Your kid thinks you are dumb.
- You worry about how to pay for college.

- Your parents help with the kids a lot.
- You worry about the kids all of the time.
- You wonder if you should move or just add on.
- Your child ruins your house with slime.
- Your child is moody and so are you at times.
- You don't know how to get Crazy Aaron's Thinking Putty out of Lululemon tights.

I hope you can relax this weekend, knowing that everything is fine and that you are "normal," at least a little bit.

Andy

• • • • • •

Teasing is good

Hello Middle School Parents!

I have decided that it is good for everyone involved. Can it be taken too far? Yes, but everything in life can, especially the fun stuff. The window of opportunity for maximum effectiveness is only about 4 years, from ages 11 to 14. Their insecurity and awkwardness are the fuel that makes this all possible. This may sound counterintuitive to the anti-bullying movement, but here it is. I think making fun of, embarrassing and teasing your kids is awesome. To make a generalization, I have observed that dads are more skilled at teasing their kids than moms. It might be the one thing we are better at if you don't include cleaning the grill and unclogging toilets. I will wager that there has been little research done on the effects of good natured teasing on the long term mental and emotional health of young children.

Here is my hypothesis: Children with parents that take the time, energy and love to tease, joke around with and embarrass their kids will end up with children who are happier, funnier, and more resilient when dealing with malicious peer teasing and other relational challenges later on in life. They know how to deal with it, how to roll with it, and have thicker skin than those who were treated with kid gloves.

When your child was born, you signed papers in the hospital giving you the right to embarrass them. This is all OK. You are funny and talented. Don't forget that. Below are a few ideas for implementing the "embarrass-annoy-love" model of child rearing:

- Use out of date lingo with vigor and frequency. "How's it poppin' big daddy? You need a hand with that jawn?"
- Talk to strangers about your kids in the presence of your kids. Example: "Excuse me sir, my daughter loves pick up trucks, can we take a look at yours?"
- Pretend you are popular. Honk the horn and wave out the car window to people you don't really know.
- Imitate them when they complain about something. Use your best middle school voice: "Oh my gosh, this food is like so gross."
- Walk around with your shirt off (this is a dad only suggestion).
- Make up stupid names for things and if they appear to be annoyed, do it more. "You guys want me to cook up my famous 18 Wheeler for breakfast?" (Two eggs sunny side up, bacon and toast.)
- Have a tag line. If you really get them annoyed or "landed a sweet bust" (you can use that too) punctuate it with something uniquely yours. Some examples might be: "Bam! Got you!" or maybe "Sizzle snap, who's the man?"

- Play music from your era loud and sing along to it when they are in the car. Remember to lock the doors, you don't want them jumping out.
- Some signs that you are doing a good job might be statements like: "Dad, you are so annoying," "You are such a dork," or "Please stop. Being with you is so embarrassing!" If they communicate you are number 1 in their book using their best non-verbal communication skills, mission accomplished!

These are all just suggestions that have worked for me in the past. You need to "make it your own, dawg."

I hope you have a wonderful weekend infused with fun, good natured teasing and laughter!

Andy

• • • • • •

Hello Middle School Parents!

Why is it so hard for middle school students to be self-advocates? By this I mean looking out for themselves, telling others what they need and how to take responsibility for their actions. Failure to do this can be extremely frustrating and confusing for parents. I am not talking about them badgering you for a new phone or telling you how stupid you are. That is called being a huge pain in the ***...self-advocacy is different. Have you ever said something like this to your child:

"Why don't you just ask the teacher for help?"

"I wish you would just talk to your coach and ask how you can improve."

"Tell him how you feel and maybe he will stop doing/saying that to you."

"Does your teacher know you have no idea what is going on in class?"

"We are going on vacation next week, have you spoken to your teachers about the work you will miss?"

"Just talk to your father and tell him you don't feel the recycling bins need to be cleaned again this week."

As adults, we know self-advocacy is critical to their success and a necessary component to navigating through life's challenges and obstacles. I have great news for you! If your kid is horrible at this or his or her self-advocacy skills are non-existent, that is totally normal! Becoming a strong self-advocate may not happen until high school or beyond. But the earlier they start practicing, the better.

Middle school students are typically poor self-advocates because:

- Their parents are awesome at it, love them and they have always done it for them. (I am talking about you.)
- It is hard to be good at something you have never done before. (The exception to this is the first time I played pickle ball. Amazing!) They are just starting to learn, so be patient!

- Lack of self-awareness. You have to know what you need before you can ask for it.
- Low confidence and being self-conscious makes speaking up and expressing yourself difficult.
- They just want to fit in and be "normal." Asking for help can make them feel vulnerable and different.

How do we get this ball rolling? The sooner your child becomes "proficient" (state testing term) in this skill the better. Below are a few ideas that might help:
- Slowly transition the role and responsibility of advocating to your child. Problem with a teacher, coach, friend, their counselor (no way!)? Talk to your child about it and help them come up with a plan of action.
- Plan what they will say and how and when they will say it. Talk about eye contact, tone of voice, and staying calm. Role playing and having some notes can help.
- Identify the support systems available. Who should they talk to? Who can help them?
- Encourage your child to set up a meeting with their teachers to discuss their progress.
- Have them talk to their counselor bearing freshly baked cookies in a decorative tin.
- Continue making suggestions you know are in their best interest even if they don't follow through. They will one day realize you do, sort of, know what you are talking about!

Wow! Another thing for the kids to work on! Middle school is not easy and figuring it all out can be tough. Hang in there and call your school counselor if you need some help. Be an advocate for yourself!

I hope you have a great weekend!

Andy

· · · · · ·

Hello Middle School Parents!

Last night I was cleaning up after dinner and listening to some country music. I started to pay attention to the words (as I scrubbed a pot with one of those smiley faced scratchy pads) and the theme I heard was about being thankful for what we have. The songs were about enjoying the moment and cherishing this time we have with our children. I think that scratchy pad started to look at me and it might have tilted it's head as if to say, "think about it"… As a generous lather formed in the pot, I realized that I have not been slowing down enough to really pay attention to everything I have to be thankful for. The next day at school I watched the smiling and happy children enter the building. It reminded me how amazing these kids are and what a gift we all have. Let's take a look at a few ideas to help us all to be thankful. This can work for our children as well! Talk to them about it:

- Journal. Take a few minutes a couple of times a week to write down what you are thankful for. I will often ask my kids, "tell me the good news!" Ask yourself the same question.
- Embrace setbacks. When things don't go the way you planned, accept it as part of the overall journey.
- Spend time with loved ones. Like the line from the country song, "suddenly fishing wasn't such an imposition." Say "yes."

- Avoid negative social media. Gossiping and putting people down drains your bucket.
- It's the small stuff. Do something nice for someone every day. Hold a door, compliment someone, smile. It all adds up.
- Volunteer. Pay it forward. Everyone needs help once in a while.
- Change one word. We often say things like, "I have to drive my kid to practice" or "I have to go to work today." Change it to "I get to." How awesome is it that your kid is healthy and can play a sport and that you have a job? The things you do every day are not burdens but opportunities.
- Practice mindfulness. Live in the here and now. Appreciate the moment. I know people speak highly of the ability to multi-task but I think that stinks. Immerse yourself in the present. I am horrible at multi-tasking. If I am chewing gum, I sit there until it loses flavor, spit it out and resume my activity. I am not kidding.
- Take a break. Take a moment to go for a walk, look at the clouds and think. Slow down!
- Say "Thank you." When you are thankful for someone, tell them.
- At dinner, ask everyone to say one thing they are thankful for. If they make a joke of it, don't feed them.

The county music finally switched themes and next week I am probably going to skip school (this is just between us, right?) to go fishing with my dog while driving a new pickup truck that I now plan to purchase! The message next week may be about poor decision making, but we shall see.

Have a happy Thanksgiving!

Andy

• • • • • •

Hello Middle School Parents!

I don't really bleed green. I am not a long-time listener, first time caller. I don't think we live in the suburbs of "Wentzadelphia" and when I hear "fly eagles fly," I am typically looking for wildlife. All this being said, my son and I go to one Philadelphia Eagles game a year and it is some of the best people watching on the planet. I aggressively navigate 95 North wearing my Nnamdi Asomugha jersey, which my son tells me is the most embarrassing jersey of all time. I eagerly pay $40 to park the car and we slowly make our way through the tailgates of old men almost playing football while holding beer cans, and into the stadium. Throughout this entire experience I find myself lacking tolerance. I realize I am passing judgement and drawing conclusions about the passionate Eagles fans whom I don't really understand. Old stereotypes I learned as a youth bubble to the surface and my level of empathy for the people around me dwindles to zero. As my empathy goes down, my frustration, anger and unwillingness to learn about this "Eagles Culture" goes up. The bad language, drunkenness and misguided passion...this is so annoying...and then the Eagles score and the fans start high fiving everyone, including me! A few seconds ago I thought that guy was a total Jackalope and now he is my buddy! I wave my Toyota Woo Hoo towel and realize I am having a great time. I am starting to understand all of this and more importantly, the people who love it. I accidently scrape my hand on the seat bracket and to my amazement, my blood does start to look a little green after all...

Below are a few tips, ideas and reminders for teaching our children tolerance. We all know this stuff, but at times, it is very easy to forget:

- What cultural stereotypes have you learned? What are your areas of weakness? Become aware of them and do your best to correct what you can.
- The kids have big ears! They are always listening to adult conversations. Be aware of jokes, and other comments that might be insensitive.
- Having tolerance does not mean that you have to be OK with poor behavior. Treating others with respect is the key here.
- People with strong self-esteem are less likely to treat others poorly. Do everything you can to provide your kids with opportunities to feel good about who they are. Place value on the differences in your own kids.
- Provide opportunities for your kids to be around people who are different from them.
- Our kids do what we do. They say what we say. Model tolerance and treat others with respect and kindness, and our kids will follow.
- Take time to learn about new cultures with your kids. Pick a night where you cook a meal from another country and talk about it as a family.

I hope you have a wonderful weekend and Go Birds!

Andy

• • • • • •

Hello Middle School Parents!

I like to collect them. Maybe save is a better word. I almost get excited when I see them. They are normally in pairs if I get to them quickly enough. Alone, they are what I call "singlets." I never knew when the time would come, when the emergency would occur. Who can predict such things? If you could they would be called "planned incidents" and not "emergencies." Either way, last Tuesday it happened, and I was rewarded for my penurious and environmentally inspired habitual ways. For an entire year, when a bar of soap would finally succumb to "the break," its strong, solid rectangular shape reduced to two thin shavings of its former self, I would lovingly save them in a bag. How long can you use two pieces of a bar of soap in the shower? When do you take the plunge and open a new one? Lazy, cheap, already wet every time you realize it and you don't want to get out of the shower? Either way, for 365 days I stood vigil, collecting the soap remnants with a master plan, a vision, of making them whole again. Using a loaf pan and boiling water, in the dark of night, I fused the eclectic mix of soaps together in the ultimate display of economical and artistic unity. A mélange of scents and textures gratefully succumbing to the heat in one last hopeful act of acquiescence. My scientific experiment resulted in what resembled a loaf of hard soapy blue cheese with beautiful veining. The soap had been reborn, ready to serve. Something out of nothing. Soup from a stone or soap from soap in this case. When the yell of, "we are totally out of soap" came ringing throughout the house, I heroically sprang into action, grateful for my planning, dedication and being a cheap son of a female dog. I handed out the rough-cut bars to my family, my pride shielding me from their confused and judgmental looks. Ungrateful and dirty children. Without options or recourse, they accepted my soapy display of thriftiness. The next shower, the next 20, 30, 40 showers were free, gloriously free, and all because of me!

Money. Spending money. Understanding money. Money, money, money. How do we teach our kids about being thrifty, wise and respectful of money? Below are a few tips and reminders that might help:

- Work. Have them really work to earn the money. Spending money that has been given to you is so easy. Spending money you earned shoveling driveways, babysitting or scrubbing toilets is much harder.
- Allowances are weird. Are you paying them for the privilege of housing, clothing and feeding them? They should be paying you! If they do real work, sure, paying them is fine. Money for nothing does not make sense.
- Bring them to the bank and open an account. Teach them how to view their balances. Point out that when they deposit that gift from grandma, the account goes up.
- Slow. If their money is in the bank, there is a speed bump between the money and impulsive purchases. Slowing down the spending process can help reduce unnecessary spending.
- Save. If they really want something, help them set up a plan to save for it. Your kid is less likely to leave their new baseball glove outside in the rain if they raked leaves for 5 hours to pay for it. I have my own kids save up for Father's Day gifts each year, all in the name of education.

- Credit cards. Explain how they work and why they stink. Your kids are old enough now to understand interest rates. You might also mention that if they sign up for a credit card on spring break when they are in college, as long as they get a free t-shirt, it is OK...
- Share some of the details. If you are out to dinner or paying for their soccer league, etc., every once in a while show them the bill. Explain it. Make sure they understand that you are paying for it. Make a point to make a point. This stuff is not free, but your soap could be...

I hope you have a wonderful weekend!

Andy

December

· · · · · ·

Hello Middle School Parents!

Well, the holiday cards started pouring in at my house with the pictures of good looking, extremely happy and well- adjusted families. Even the dogs look great. Lab or Labradoodle? Wow, were they on vacation in the Bahamas? Nice. It was at this moment that my wife and I realized we did not have our own card finished! We put in jeopardy our way of communicating our marital and emotional success to everyone we care about (and sort of care about). Was free shipping still available? Why didn't we take more pictures of the kids together this summer? The holiday stress had found its way into our home!! What to do?

All of the articles I have read about reducing holiday stress say stuff like don't eat or drink excessively. Exercise, forgive people, don't spend too much money and be nice. This all sounds good but let's face it, how often do you get to eat honey baked ham, and the holiday cookies are pure bite sized joy. How can you go for a jog with snow on the road, your nasty neighbor is unforgivable, and truthfully, that egg nog your aunt makes is worth another cup? (Does she put lighter fluid in that?) Let's pull it together here. Ok, here are some tips for keeping the family running on all 8 cylinders this holiday season:

- Don't be afraid to say "no" to parties or other obligations that you honestly don't want to attend.
- Get plenty of sleep and try to make an effort to eat at least one healthy meal a day.
- Schedule down time and put it on your calendar to make sure it happens.
- Be fully present and connect with your kids and spouse. (Don't address cards while watching *The Polar Express* with your family!)
- Take care of yourself. Make time to do the normal things that make you happy and relaxed. Yoga, reading, walking etc. You matter too!
- Laugh as much as you can! Try this: at the dinner table, take turns allowing the kids to tell a joke. The rule is, everyone laughs a lot even if the joke isn't funny. Fake laughing leads to real laughing!
- With your family, write down the top five holiday events, activities, or traditions that are the most meaningful to you. You can then use this list as the filter through which you make decisions about which traditions to keep and which to lose. For example, if nobody in your family cares about holiday lights in the yard, don't bother putting them up.
- Basically, if you don't enjoy it, if it does not bring you and your family joy, think about cutting it out!

- Preserve the things that are authentic and help to cultivate love and happiness. This is the good stuff.

I hope you have a relaxing and fun holiday season!

Andy

• • • • • •

Hello Middle School Parents!

What are the things that cause stress for your children? In my conversations with students this past week, I noticed a few general reoccurring themes that I think are worth mentioning. The more aware we are of the sources of stress in our children, the more we can do to help alleviate it. Below are a few things to keep in mind:

- Parents' expectations: Make sure to have realistic expectations for your children. Expecting "all A's" is not reasonable for most kids. Base your assessment of your children on their work ethic and commitment to school. If the end result is a hard earned B, count that as a win. The perceived pressure from parents can be intense. It is important to remember they are processing the messages you send through the eyes of a sensitive, insecure adolescent. It is for that very reason that you are "always yelling" at them.
- Social media: They feel obligated to it. For many it is a burden that they don't feel empowered to pull away from. Many students have reported when, for whatever reason, they are not able to use their phone, they feel liberated. Snap Chat and Insta-

50

gram have become highways for social conflict, bullying and overall sadness. Keep close tabs on your child's phone usage. Insider tip: look at the timestamp on the Instagram messages they sent. Past their bed time? Probably. Even better, enable features that restrict the times they can use their phones.

- Sleep: Many of our students are not getting enough sleep. Just this week three separate students reported that they were up past 12 on their phones with friends!
- Activities: Keeping a commitment to activities outside of school can be fantastic. Always keep the fun factor in mind. Is their activity still fun? Do they enjoy it? Is it helping to reduce stress or contributing to it. Ask them.
- School work: The kids are getting more homework now. The honeymoon period is over. This year many students report that they have more consistent homework. While they feel more prepared, the quantity and the time required to complete the work can be challenging. Please keep in mind that if your child is having difficulty with work completion, organization or time management, your school counselor can help!
- Self-doubt: They are insecure. Many are struggling daily with the peer pressure to climb the social ladder at great expense. The social maneuvering is a constant and relentless undercurrent that can and does undermine their ability to cope with their stress.

Speaking of self-doubt, there is a dance next week!

Andy

. . . . . .

Hello Middle School Parents!

The dance is tonight from 7:30 – 9:30!

The first time I chaperoned a middle school dance, something was in the air and it was thick and heavy. Was it steam or perhaps indoor fog? The closer I got to the gym I realized what it was. Hormones! I felt like Scooby Doo in a graveyard. Confused and afraid, I just wanted to run away. Luckily, the soothingly familiar rhythmic beat of The Chicken Dance brought me back to my job of helping to supervise 200 nervous, self-conscious kids in a dimly lit gym. If I was apprehensive about this experience, how must the kids feel? Below are a few tips to help make their first middle school dance amazing!

- Smile: Make them smile. Not to make them happy, but to see how much trash is caught in their braces. If you have a Waterpik that can help clean out the debris, but a power washer on a low setting can work as well.
- Acne check: Give them a good look to make sure they don't have a major growth on their face. Look even closer for any "up and coming" zits that may emerge in the next few hours.
- Bathroom: Remind them not to hang out in the bathroom. While it may provide a temporary safe haven from dancing, it is not where they are going to have fun. Studies have shown that if you stay in a bathroom for more than 5 minutes, the odors seep into your clothing.

- Nerves: The other kids are just as nervous as they are. If others look more confident, they are just better actors. Everyone in the room, including the chaperones, are nervous.
- Dance: Encourage you child to dance and not just sit around the perimeter doing nothing. Be a good role model and show your kids some of your best moves. You know you have one. The Worm, The Sprinkler, whatever your specialty dance move is, demonstrate it for your kids. Feel free to do this at the actual dance. They will love you for it.
- Scent: Before they depress the button that releases the toxic odor of their choice, remind them that a little cologne, perfume, whatever, goes a long way.
- Slow dance: The slow dance is the grand daddy event of a middle school dance. This is where the rubber meets the road. Who has the courage to ask someone to dance? If you child is one the brave few, remind them not to make eye contact with their friends on the sidelines. They will do everything in their power to mess with them. Stay focused on the task at hand!
- Behavior: Their overall behavior choices should be made as if the principal and their grandmother were intently watching their every move.
- Fun: Remind them to have fun. Middle school dances are memories that can last a lifetime!

I hope you have a wonderful weekend!

Andy

• • • • • •

Hello Middle School Parents!

Think back to college. Did you ever spend time with a friend late at night and they said ridiculous things? They cried, they laughed, and you knowingly humored them, took care of them, and waited for the episode to pass. You were able to do this with a smile, perhaps because you knew they were mentally compromised at the time. You knew they didn't really mean it. If you haven't already figured it out, your kids are out of their minds too and yes, you need to take care of them! They are intoxicated with a cocktail of hormones, insecurity and mood swings. Middle school children, much like your college friend, will come home and say the most alarming things to their parents. If those same words were uttered by an adult or any other non-adolescent (sane person), swift and severe action would need to be taken to correct or fix the problem. In most cases with middle school students, a slower, calmer approach to the "emergency" is best.

Some alarming things parents have reported that their children have said to them recently are:

- "I hate school."
- "I don't have any friends at school."
- "I am failing all of my classes."
- "I hate you!" (Meaning their parents.)
- "This dinner you made is gross."
- "Everyone is mean to me."

Here are a few tips and reminders for dealing with these highly emotional and alarming outbursts that are often accompanied by disrespectful behavior:

- Stay calm!
- Listen and listen some more (and don't laugh if they really sound crazy).
- With social drama, don't get involved and start calling other parents. This is a last resort only.
- Don't take it personally. Remember they are "under the influence of adolescence."
- Remind yourself they don't mean it. Say it over and over to yourself like a meditation mantra.
- This is common adolescent behavior. It is not just your kid! Your neighbor's kid, now they have problems!
- Perception is reality... their perception is way off so how they see the problem most likely is too. Help them identify the actual facts to refocus their perceptions, much like a detective. "Just the facts, ma'am."
- Correct their rude behavior in a matter of fact kind of way. Don't get emotional. "Mom, this dinner stinks!" "Thank you for the feedback Beavis. Now please go to your room."
- Don't get lazy and let their inappropriate behavior slide. Ignoring it is so nice and easy, until it isn't.
- Whatever the emergency or problem is, remind yourself this is most likely temporary.
- Action is probably not necessary. In many cases, the problem will work itself out (it's like being constipated, but different).
- They are acting disrespectful with you because they love you and know they are safe with you.
- In the event that a problem is long lasting (a few weeks or more) and real, seeking help or dealing with it in a more direct manner is appropriate.
- Their problems are very real to them. Your job is to respect their feelings and listen.

I hope you have a wonderful weekend!

Andy

• • • • • •

Hello Middle School Parents!

My wife suggested that I get my hearing checked. Apparently, I "can't hear anything she says." Being the compliant husband that I am, I agreed that having a medical professional assess the situation was indeed a good idea. Perhaps I do have a hearing issue. Maybe I have what Shrek had when he pulls candles out of his ears. The weird thing is, I can hear some things and not others. When I was informed that my mother-in-law was coming over for dinner, somehow this did not register with me. Was I running the leaf blower when she said that? There was a request to pick up some paper towels from the grocery store; again, I totally missed it. Strangely enough, when we were talking about how good the bacon was at breakfast I could hear every word. The problem gets worse. I think there could be some genetic loading. Last night, all three of my children were unable to hear me ask them to pick up their clothes and put them down the laundry chute. What is going on? Alas, perhaps some mysteries are best left unsolved...

My older son said something at dinner the other night. I responded positively with "that is such a good idea!" My 6th grade daughter replied with, "Seriously Dad? I just said the same thing a few minutes ago. You were not listening!" She was totally right! Listening and actually hearing are two different things. I had grown so accustomed to half listening/humoring the child like things she

56

said in the past, that I neglected to realize she was "turning the cognitive corner," finding her voice and really needed to be heard. Here are a few tips and reminders for communicating with your children (and spouse?) and possibly avoiding a trip to the audiologist:

- Trick them. If you really want your child to talk with you, they can't realize that is what you are doing. Make the talking something that happens when you are doing something fun with them. Playing basketball, cooking, cleaning the bathroom, whatever is relaxing and enjoyable.
- Small doses. If they are talking about something serious, it is OK to follow their lead and take a break from that topic. They will come back to it when they are ready. It can be easier to talk about serious stuff a little at a time.
- Avoid sitting them down to officially talk. They have seen too many Sponge Bob episodes and other shows where weird counselors (and there are a lot of them) try to get kids to talk.
- Simply listen. Resist the urge to talk. Often kids just want to talk and vent. You don't have to have the answers.
- When appropriate, act on their suggestions and ideas. Show them you value their opinion.
- Ask them their opinion on the family decisions you are trying to make. Include them.
- If they are talking, pay attention. Put down the phone, book (unless you are reading this one) and listen.
- Reflect back what they are saying to check for understanding.

- Minimal encouragers. "Yes," "OK." Nod your head in understanding. Send the message that you get it. (Warning: doing too much of this is really weird.)
- Keep your cool. If your kid tells you something they did, or a bad decision they made, don't get angry. The second you show anger, they will totally shut down. "I am sorry to hear you covered your sister's entire room and the dog in shaving cream. Can you tell me more about that?"

Can you hear me, or do I need to speak up?

I hope you have a wonderful weekend!

Andy

• • • • • •

Holiday Madness

Hello Middle School Parents!

I was expecting a hero's welcome. Visions of hugs, praise and other overtures of unbridled appreciation blurred my vision on the drive home. In the back of my pickup truck I had not one, but two Christmas trees! Unprompted, and independent of any directive, I took the initiative to purchase a tree for my family as well as for my parents. I felt like Kris Kringle himself. The natural high from doing something good was coursing through my body. I deftly maneuvered the tree into the house with minimal branch and needle shaving on the door jamb. My adoring wife was certainly waiting for her Christmas Knight in flannel armor to return. Would she greet me with a fresh cup of eggnog or a kiss? Perhaps both? I leaned the tree against the window as she entered the room. "You got the plastic netting on the tree? You know that stuff kills tur-tles." "Were all of the trees this small? All of the kids or-naments are not going to fit." My mouth open, heart pounding, I scanned the room for the fresh eggnog and mistletoe. Nothing. I kept quiet. After years of training I knew less was more. With the help of our children, we positioned the tree into the stand. "You should have had them trim more off the bottom. It won't sit flush on the stand." Again, I laid low. Underneath the tree, I clipped a few more strategic branches, and tightened the screws on the stand as my wife instructed my son to let go of the tree. Still laying on my stomach, I noticed the festive red legs of the tree stand starting to pull away from the ground. The resentful tree, in a vengeful last move, slowly enveloped me and I started to smile. Was this the hug I was expecting? There were faint muffled sounds of people yelling and dogs barking. To my surprise, I had found a quiet, welcoming pine scented respite from the holiday madness...

On another note, the winter concert was amazing! Our 5th and 6th graders did such a wonderful job. The chorus sang "My Favorite Things," which is a beautiful and festive song. I took the liberty of modifying the lyrics. I hope you enjoy!

<u>"My Favorite (Middle School) Things"</u>
Tater Tots with Ketchup
And children are crazy
Attitude and eye rolls and kids that are lazy
Mood swings and hormones tied up with strings
These are few of my favorite things

Cream-colored Ugg boots and North Face Jackets
Class bells and hall smells

And slime with math packets
Wet toilet paper they throw and or fling
These are a few of my favorite things

When the boys cry
When the girls fight
When they feel so sad
I simply remember winter break is in sight
And then I don't feel so bad!

Remember to laugh and have as much fun as you can during the holiday season!

I hope you have a wonderful weekend!

Andy

• • • • • •

Hello Middle School Parents!

When do you normally sit down and think, "How can I be a better parent to my middle school student?" Maybe you do that in between going to work and doing the laundry, or while picking up after the dog in the yard. Does your phone make a noise reminding you that between 12-1 on Thursday you are going to ponder ways to better support your children? You probably often find yourself saying "Sorry Sally, I can't go out to dinner with you on Saturday, I am brainstorming ways to improve as a parent. Maybe next time!"… Oh, you don't do that? (Insert judgmental tone and eye rolling from this author.) Hmmm, I think we have some work to do with you. The good news is there is a new year just around the corner! How about this: On

New Year's Eve, instead of playing Cards Against Humanity or Twister with your friends, you can suggest that everyone come up with 5 of the most important social and emotional skills for your kids to focus on next year and share them with the group? I suspect you might not get invited back to the party next year, but there is a price to pay for everything I guess...

More good news! I have decided to do the work for you! It is sort of like getting prepared food at the grocery store but way less money. Below you will find a few things that in my estimation would be admirable goals to discuss or at least keep in mind for your middle school child in the new year:

- Managing Friends: Middle school is plagued with a very obvious and defined social ladder. The kids all know who is "popular" and who is not. Often, if given an opportunity, some children will vie for a seat at the popular table at the expense of their real friends. Remind your children that real friends are kind and accept them for who they are. Real friends make them feel good and are nice; they treat them the way they want to be treated.
- Self-Advocacy: Encourage your child to speak for themselves, even if you are pretty sure they won't do it or will mess it up. The sooner they start asking for help and communicating what they need the better!
- Time management: The kids are busy. They will continue to have more academic demands placed on them as they progress through middle school. Making a deliberate and intentional plan for how they use their time can be very helpful. If you see your child wasting an excessive amount of

time and then freaking out because they have school work due or tests they are not prepared for, they may need to focus on this.

- Figuring out how to study: Some students have difficulty in school and the need to study hard has always been a necessary skill for them. Other students can listen in class and get solid grades with little or no studying. These are the kids that don't know how to study. Learning how to study is a process, an evolution if you will, that takes time. Encourage your child to start now by trying different strategies so they can figure out what works for them.

- Taking control of their emotions: Learning how to express their feelings through talking, journaling, etc. combined with the implementation of daily stress reducing strategies (exercise, art, reading, music and more) are the key components to becoming a master of one's emotions. The sooner they start the better!

Check the box! You are done. A fully prepared middle school parenting to do list for the new year. Now, get out that Twister board and have fun!

I hope you have a wonderful winter break!

Andy

January

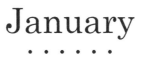

Hello Middle School Parents!

What do the "The A-Team," the 1927 Yankees, the 1972 Miami Dolphins, The Great Pyramid of Giza, and Ben and Jerry have in common? They all accomplished unique and amazing things, in large part, because they worked as high-performance teams. While BA Baracus (Mr. T) was an accomplished van driver and most likely could help carry 1.5 ton blocks of limestone for the pyramid, he might have had a difficult time developing Chunky Monkey. Conversely, Ben and Jerry probably don't believe in violence (even to protect the innocent) and ride eco-friendly bikes, not high-performance vans. So different and yet similar... Either way, "The A Team" (and the rest of the not as cool teams I mentioned above) were all well-oiled machines working in unison to achieve a common goal. The A-Team's accomplishments were tremendous and by all historical accounts, true. I can't vouch for the pyramid

as that sounds ridiculous. (Remember, if you have a problem, if no one else can help, and if you can find them,
maybe you can hire the A-Team.) The point is, working as
a team can produce fantastic results, much greater than
the sum of the parts. What are the components of a strong
team and, most importantly how can we apply this to raising our own family?

- Your family is very much your "A-Team" and you
  are in charge. (If you are having trouble getting into
  this role, put a bunch of gold chains around the
  neck of your kid and dangle a cigar from your
  mouth while giving the orders.)
- Too often members of a family only work independently. Dad and Mom work all day doing their
  thing, the kids go to school and sports, etc. and they
  all come together at the end of the day. This independent contractor type of living does not always
  leverage the benefits of a team.
- If you are not working as a team, your level of understanding and empathy for each other can go
  down. You don't really know what your spouse does
  at work or what the kids are doing at school. Without some intentional and thoughtful team building
  opportunities, these relational gaps can widen, at
  times accented with misplaced judgement. ("What
  do you do all day anyway??")
- Find opportunities to create a common goal.
  Whether it is working on a project, shoveling snow,
  designing a new addition, working on a puzzle,
  planning dinners, baking cookies for your child's
  counselor, or implementing a plan to save money on
  electricity. Whatever it is, do your best as the head
  coach to get buy-in from the other team members
  on something you can all work on together.

- Set some clear goals and give everyone a defined role that they play.
- Set a good example by clearly communicating with everyone.
- By working on something as a family, it is an opportunity to access the new capabilities of your children. Give them new, challenging responsibilities and see how they do. (I am not suggesting you ask them to re-shingle the garage, or run the table saw, but that is your call.)
- The trick to this is making the time to work together and making it fun! The vacation coming up might be the perfect time.

I hope you have a wonderful weekend!

Andy

• • • • • •

Midlife crisis

Hello Middle School Parents!

I am going to make you feel even older than you look. I apologize in advance for pointing out a few facts of life. (You take the good, you take the bad, you take them both and there you have, The Facts of Life, The Facts of Life…that was a good show. Tootie was cool and I almost married Blair but my 5th grade teacher talked me out of it…)

Here are a few observations that made me stop and think, so I thought I would share them with you:

- Many parents are between 35 – 45 when their first child enters adolescence.

- There is evidence that between the ages of 35-45 can be a difficult time for many adults. Have you ever thought about buying a motorcycle, new sports car, dropping everything and moving to Vermont, quitting your job to start a food truck while living in a yurt? Perhaps you are experiencing a "mid-life crisis." Awesome.

- What this means is that both you and your child are going through a lot of significant changes at the same time!

- Your kids are entering a period of rapid growth. They are getting stronger, faster, and smarter. They are maturing and approaching the prime of their lives. You (and me) on the other hand are buying pants with hidden elastic waist bands, drinking smoothies and purchasing age defying ointments made from the larva of the African Tulip Bug.

- They view life time in terms of how long they have been on this earth, while we view it as how much time we have left. Adolescents tend to think about their future, which seems unlimited, while adults' views of the future may have less possibilities and be more limited. (I am not saying you can't go back to school and become a veterinarian, backpack through Europe with your buddy or move back into your old fraternity house. That might still happen...)

- Adolescents are on the threshold of becoming adults, making choices, and gaining power and status as they reach goals and milestones in relationships and occupations. For us, we have already made many important choices in our lives that we now live with, good and bad. For example, I purchased a John Deere lawn mower (I call it a tractor and it makes me feel tough. I also got a free "owners" hat) 20 years ago and it is still fantastic today. I also went to college, got married, had kids, and entered into a career, blah, blah, blah... the tractor is really awesome, did I mention that?

- Why do we think about the consequences of our actions and our kids often don't? It appears that all of that extra fat adults carry around also acts as insulation to the nerves in our brains that connect our frontal lobes. So keep eating! This is the part of the brain that controls our "judgement," and it is not fully developed in teens.

Being aware that we are at dramatically different life stages than our children can help us to understand and explain why we see the world through such a different lens. Parents may be more conservative then their kids. Kids get annoyed at parents' constant attention. Their journey for independence can be so stressful for us and act as a beacon, signaling the last stage of our career as parents. Keeping some of this in mind can help us to be more understanding parents and perhaps more appreciative of this amazing time we have with our family and our children. Honestly, you still look good! You still have what it takes and you are going places...you might just get there faster on a Harley!

Andy

• • • • • •

Dating

Hello Middle School Parents!

Did you hear about Joe and Sally? You didn't? Seriously? Joe asked her out and she said "yes!" Joe had Sam check with Lucy and Lucy told Sam that Sally thought Joe was cute! He is also very popular but that is not at all why she likes him. The problem is Myrtle texted Joe and now Sally is big time mad and she may be breaking up with Joe. Cutest couple ever, at least for now. They might get married...this is what I think I heard Fred tell Brandon in health class. The real news is however, that Joanie loves Chachi, but you don't know them. They go to private school...

Some kids in middle school are totally interested in romantic relationships. It can be nothing short of all-consuming. Other kids would rather have discussions about ponies, unicorns and Legos. Either and both are totally normal.

In the event that your child is on the brink or fully immersed in relationships, here are a few things for you to think about:

- Don't make fun of your child for their feelings about their relationships. Their feelings are new and real. It is very tempting to make a joke about it because what they say and do can appear to be ridiculous. They are total rookies at this whole guy/girl thing so cut them a break.
- By taking their feelings seriously, you will encourage communication between you and your child, hopefully keeping you somewhat in the loop.
- If they are in a relationship, talk with them openly about your views on sex, dating, and relationships in general. This can be awkward, but you have to do it. Very similar to cleaning out the recycling bins (they look great, by the way!)
- If the person they are dating is not a felon, dealing drugs, or part of one of those tough preppy gangs

like the "Golfing Gangsters" or the especially nasty "Vineyard Vine Vandals" (we all have different criteria for acceptability) let your child take the lead on the relationship. Keep a close eye on things and talk with them as necessary. If your child is dishonest, breaks your rules, etc., you will need to step in. Otherwise let the relationship run its course, similar to dealing with a virus.

- If you actually like the person they are dating, it is OK to let the kids know it. If the kids are treating each other in a respectful and appropriate way, tell them. You want to encourage and acknowledge healthy relational behaviors.

- If things do go south, and the kids are breaking the rules, make sure to keep the other parents informed. You would want to know, so do they.

- Make your child aware if you see them out of balance with their time, if they start to neglect their friends, sports, hobbies etc. they may need some redirection.

- Don't allow the kids to be home alone without a responsible adult around.

- Always call the other parents when your child sets up a sleep over at his or her friend's house. This can be used as an alibi for an "unauthorized" get together.

- Prepare yourself for tears. There will be breakups. The best medicine is distraction. Take them to dinner or the movies. Get them out of the house and moving.

- Take time to remember your first love and bring yourself back to that age. Having empathy and understanding is the best way you can help your child.

I hope you have a great weekend!

Andy

• • • • • •

Hello Middle School Parents!

Perhaps it was the time the student decided to climb on the roof of the school to retrieve a kick ball. Or maybe when the student made "smoogies" (wet toilet paper balls) with all the toilet paper (4.5 miles worth if stretched end to end) in the bathroom and did some redecorating. I can't forget Jimmy. Jimmy thought it was a good idea (this is before cell phones) to photo copy pictures from a magazine not intended for children and sell the copies for $1 each out of his locker. Entrepreneurial yes, a good decision no. (I think he is now VP of Sales for a Fortune 500 company.) The point is, middle schoolers are notorious for making impulsive, bad decisions! Previously I spoke about frontal lobes and since I thought it made me sound smart, I am going to continue in this vein.

The good news is that decision-making abilities improve over the course of adolescence. It is only going to get better! Let's take a closer look at the skills that are developing:

- The ability to take multiple points of view into consideration and compare them. (For example, you think wearing what appears to be a small napkin as a skirt to the mall is a bad idea, while her best friends thinks it is "hot.")
- Being able to think in hypothetical terms. This helps them to possibly consider the long-term consequences of their actions. (Jimmy was eager to

make $15 in 3 minutes before homeroom but getting suspended was not on his radar. More developing needed.)

- Being able to look ahead and determine risks and likely outcomes. (Stealing the golf carts and driving around with my buddies is going to be awesome...until I crash into the stream and get caught.)

- Recognizing the value in asking for another opinion on something they are thinking about; the opinions of other people hold more weight than that of parents. (Should I take 15 AP level classes next year? My parents can't even spell AP so I will ask my counselor.)

- Peer pressure and the urge to conform is highest at the middle school level. It is for this reason that the kids often dress, talk and act alike. This can impact decision making in both good and bad ways. Because I have worked in middle school for so long, I find myself wearing Uggs while selfishly and chronically snap chatting with my friends. My wife gets annoyed. Come to think of it, I have not seen her for some time now...

- The kids will slowly acquire the necessary skills to make good choices. It takes time and copious amounts of redirection, discussion, patience and laughter from all of the adults that work to raise our children!!

And listen, if you have an extra $1, I have a such a deal for you!

Andy

• • • • • •

Hello Middle School Parents!

Crisco is really slippery. So slippery in fact that I was unable to climb the light post at the intersection of Cottman and Frankford. Most would agree Crisco is a necessary evil to attain the flakiest of pie crusts but used as a pole climbing deterrent is new to me. What a cool multi-use item. Maybe this fully hydrogenated vegetable shortening now falls into the magical category of baking soda, borax, vinegar, zip ties and WD-40; a panacea for what ails you. Most of the time, one of these ingredients will be the answer to whatever problem life throws your way. Stain on your shirt, insect problem, rusty hinge, clogged toilet, smelly shoes, gum in your hair – I think that is a complete list of problems one might encounter – all can be solved with the ingredients above. I may even try Crisco as a sun block this summer. I will let you know how that goes.

OK, back to the greased pole. The Eagles big win on Sunday was a Philadelphians dream come true. The genuine excitement and joy was overwhelming. So overwhelming that attempting to climb light posts was on the menu of reasonable options as an appropriate outlet for this joy. Maybe joy is not the right word. Passion. Passion is what I saw in the Eagles fans. A focused, intense, sincere, love for a football team.

When I worked as a high school counselor, passion was also a word associated with getting into college. Schools all want to know what applicants are "passionate" about. It often seemed like if you didn't rank #1 in the state for whatever or help invent some cure for cancer, the kids *erroneously* felt they were unaccomplished and a borng high school student with an uninspired lack of direction and purpose. I don't really like the word passion in the context of raising children. It is limiting, intense, stressful and unreasonable in many cases. Is it so bad for a kid to like a bunch of stuff and be pretty good at it, maybe not "great?" Some might argue this is a healthy, happy alternative to being laser focused on perfecting one talent. How can we as parents encourage healthy exploration, personal growth, and help our children identify their interests? Below are a few ideas and reminders to consider:

- Your kid is not you and you are not your kid. Living vicariously through your child is a bad idea. It can turn you into one of those parents that yells and screams on the sidelines... you know who I mean.
- Share your interests with your child. Teach, observe and listen to them. Are they having fun? Is it a good match for their interests and abilities?
- Keep an open mind. If your child wants to learn to play the bassoon and you think that is a type of monkey, that is OK. Let them try it!
- When they no longer want to do a particular activity, it does not mean you are a quitter. Exploration and trial and error are all part of a healthy process. (Encouraging your child to finish out the season or the lessons you paid for is all within reason.)
- Take advantage of the village. If you have a buddy who knows how to weld, a relative that is amazing at fly fishing, or a neighbor that can sew, get them to spend time with your child! I know you are awesome, but you can't be good at everything!
- Learn together. You can teach an old dog new tricks. I am not calling you old or a dog (unless you

are an Eagles Underdog!) Learn something new with your child. Explore together!

- Don't judge. Even if you think something is "stupid" or "weird" if your kid enjoys it and it is healthy, roll with it. Just because you don't like it doesn't mean your kid shouldn't.
- I know it is nice when the kids are quiet, but becoming accomplished at playing video games is not a healthy interest. Put in the time with your children!
- Passion. Encourage your child to be passionate about the Eagles for the next two weeks. In place of saying "I love you" each day consider replacing that with "Go Birds!" Just an idea...

Insider Tip: If you plan to try and climb a greased lamp post after the Eagles win the super bowl, I recommend working out with a Thigh Master until the big day. It's all about the thighs!

I hope you have a wonderful weekend!

Andy

• • • • • •

Sadness

Hello Middle School Parents!

You have to be wondering if you are alone. Is something wrong? There must be. This new strange behavior coupled with intense unpredictability causes a parental terror that can be debilitating. Silence is safe. Don't tell anyone what is going on. This is a family problem of such proportions that to reveal the essence of the issue would be socially damning, spawning an onslaught of judgement from friends and family. Something has happened to your child that you are unable to explain. The profound feelings of isolation, loss, despair and confusion can only be found in one special place.

You bought a ticket to this place 10-12 years ago. Don't you remember? It was beautiful, noisy and wrapped in a blue and white striped blanket. You were tired but happy at the time of "purchase." Still don't remember? My dear guests! I am Mr. Mullen, your host. Welcome to Adolescent Island! Smiles everyone, smiles! Yes, my friends, you are currently and thankfully only temporarily, on a vacation to what is known as Adolescent Island. This is a magical place adorned with an all you can eat buffet for every meal. Some more noteworthy items on the menu are mood swings, anger, crying, yelling, unidentified sadness, and the signature dish of disrespectful behavior finished with a sprinkling of attitude…I hope you enjoy your stay!

This past week I have spoken with many distraught middle schoolers. The theme was so consistent. Sadness. The children are confused by the strong adolescent emotions. They are sad and they don't know why. I am suspecting that many of you have seen this with your child, and if you have not, stay tuned. I have good news. This is totally normal. Feeling sad at this age is to be expected, and as a parent, it can be confusing and difficult to deal with. Here are a few tips and reminders for helping you to manage your child's new and powerful feelings:

- Be patient. Don't lose your cool. Remind yourself they are under a lot of stress and confused. They can't help it.
- Remind them being sad for a short period of time is normal and OK. It is all part of growing up.

- There does not have to be a reason for being sad. They just are and that is OK.
- Let the emotions run their course. When they are crying, or yelling, let them get it out of their system. Avoid saying things like "stop crying." Go to the shed and change the oil in your lawnmower instead.
- Don't panic. Your child will be OK. It can be so painful to see your child sad, but stay positive.
- If your child is sad for what seems to be an unreasonable amount of time, please call your school counselor. There are instances when children need help.
- Remember these are new and difficult feelings for your child to manage and they are not good at it. It is similar to you trying to ride a Razor Scooter. You are out of control and have no idea what you are doing.
- Your child from many vantage points will appear to be temporarily insane and this is OK.
- When you feel like crying, try laughing instead. If you step back, their antics can be very funny.

Each morning, if I listen closely as the school buses start to arrive, I can hear someone, somewhere enthusiastically yelling, "Da Bus, Da Bus!" Just another day on Adolescent Island!

Andy

· · · · · ·

Hello Middle School Parents!

"Oh my gosh, I love them so much! I don't know why but I love all of my friends. They are always there for me. I think I am going to cry." The student who said this reminded me of how insanely passionate adolescents can be toward their friends and how totally insane they can appear to adults. The influx of emotions surrounding their friends can at times overcome the levy and flood your home and this school. I am thankful for this as it contributes to my job security. This new type of emotionally intense friendship seems to hit fast and out of the blue, very much like the current barf virus going around or perhaps a great white shark feeding on a wounded small toothed Beluga whale. When they were younger, friendships mainly focused on shared activities and things they enjoyed doing together. Now these friendships are loaded like an emotional diaper and can be every bit as messy. Let's take a closer look at a few characteristics of this new type of intimate friendship that our kids may be experiencing:

- Friendships morph into this emotionally charged, highly personal and complicated essential element of life.
- Friendships are formed through emotional connections, caring about each other and understanding one another in a special way.
- Adolescents have an overall concern for each other and a desire to share personal and sensitive information with each other.
- Relationships are open, honest and based on trust...if they are not that is when the problems start and the diaper rips.

- An increase in a desire to form relationships with opposite sex peers. (Watching their novice interactions here at school is a special treat.)
- Advances in thinking or social cognition allow adolescents to understand and communicate with each other in a more effective way.
- They are able to respond to each other's feelings and have higher levels of empathy.
- A desire for independence and the capacity to spend many hours communicating and talking with each other.
- Don't worry if your child has yet to form this type of relationships with their peers. All kids are different, and they are ready when they are ready. Typically, this is easier to see in girls than boys. Boys may appear to have the emotional intelligence of the contents of a diaper, but don't let this fool you.

My wife tells me that I act like a middle schooler. I think she must be referring to my empathy, communication skills and my overall concern for her wants and needs and not that I like diaper jokes.

I hope you have a wonderful weekend!

Andy

February

· · · · · ·

Hello Middle School Parents!

The power can be overwhelming. A burden of unparalleled proportions that has the stealthy ability to consume one's heart and soul. The allure, the promise, the responsibility. It starts out in a calm controlled manner, slowly, methodically, luring you in with tantalizing power and ability. The greatness is obvious and so is your dependence. An endless wave of new and impressive capabilities beseeches you daily. Over time, it becomes your love, your "precious" if you will. You must have it near you, with you. If lost, reason is replaced by a flood of emotion infused with anger and blame. It is part of you and you a part of it. But you are the master. You have control, or does it have control over you? You have harnessed this power for good. Your future with this powerful partner is bright...

Bilbo and Frodo Baggins from the Lord of Rings were in a similar situation. They were 3-foot-tall Hobbits with hairy toes carrying an all-powerful evil ring forged in the depths of Mordor. You, and maybe your middle school child, are humans, with hairy toes, carrying cell phones forged in the bowels of the Apple factories. If Apple came out with an i-Ring this analogy would be even easier! Frodo was trying to destroy the evil ring, while you are trying to upgrade your cell phone... your "precious."

Ahhh!!!! The cell phone dilemma for middle school students. Below are some of my highly opinionated and biased thoughts coupled with some common sense reminders about cell phones for middle school children:

- Myth Buster #1: Regardless of what you child tells you, "everyone" does not have a cell phone, especially in 5th and 6th grade.
- Myth Buster #2: You don't need a cell phone to do middle school homework.
- Middle school kids are enamored, intrigued, at least partially interested in the topics covered in sex education. In a matter of 5 seconds they can view incredibly inappropriate things. Help them by activating restricted internet access.
- When we were in school, kids could tease you but when you got home it was safe. The "bullying" ended. With phones, the harassing can continue all night long. Consider limited cell phone access when they are at home.
- The kids know more about the phones than we do. They can hide what they don't want us to see. Have open discussions with your child about how they are using their phone.

- Be a positive role model for appropriate phone etiquette. When driving, eating dinner, talking in person to someone, checking out at the grocery store, etc.
- Many issues stem from video and camera capabilities (you can only imagine what they take pictures of...) Talk to your cell phone provider and learn what your options are for disabling these features.
- With a cell phone, it only takes one lapse in judgement to negatively impact a child for the rest of their life.
- Many students have told me they feel a sense of relief when their parents take their cell phone. The social expectations are a burden for many students.
- If/when you take the cell phone, i-Pad or whatever technology away from your child and then they act crazy, out of character, angry or sad, this could be an indicator that they need a longer break from it.
- Have you ever heard that middle school students can be impulsive, immature, confused, self-centered and insecure? Does a cell phone sound like it will pair well with that? Like a nice chardonnay with a white fish poached in coconut cream finished with fresh parsley?

People will look back on this era of cell phone usage and ask, "You thought it was OK for middle school kids to have cell phones? Were you crazy??" We are currently in the Wild, Wild West of cell phones.

I hope you have a wonderful, cell phone free weekend!

Andy

· · · · · ·

Hello Middle School Parents!

It was 1980 something, and as you will all vividly remember, Tito Santana had recently won the World Wrestling Federation Intercontinental Championship in a steel cage match. Epic. Tito had perfected the "drop kick," a move where you jump into the air and kick the other guy with both feet. I had mastered this as well. One day, to my parents' delight, I was wrestling with my older brother on their bed and instinctively executed and landed a drop kick, sending my brother careening into my mother's dresser, her curling iron and well-appointed glass tray of perfume crashing to the ground. Amazed at my skill but horrified at the disaster, I ran out to the front yard. My brother grabbed his tightly packed pillow nun chucks he had made in 8th grade sewing class (for just such an occasion), and proceeded to deftly beat his chubby, red, younger brother (me) to a crying pulp under the serene beauty of a flowering cherry tree. Our neighbors, the Cranes, watched in amazement from their bay window while celebrating Passover with their family. Here are a few ideas my parents could have used to help their aspiring Tito Santana avoid a public beating and more importantly deal with our sibling rivalry that had gone unchecked:

- Most of the time, both of the kids are responsible in some way if they are fighting. Don't worry about trying to figure out who is more to blame. Don't be the referee. Punish them all! Keep it consistent and administer the discipline in equal proportions. For example, "OK boys, you were both fighting. Luckily, we have two recycling bins. You each get one to clean!"

- If you sense your kids are angry or have strong negative feelings about their sibling, give them a chance to express it. It is Ok for them to get mad, we all do from time to time. Let them know it is normal to have these feelings and give them an opportunity to talk about it.
- If you can, let the kids try and figure things out for themselves. Monitor the situation and if it gets too out of hand or there is a major imbalance of power, yes, step in. If, however they can come to a resolution on their own, it is a good life skill.
- Avoid comparing your kids. This drives them crazy and fuels resentment. Saying things like, "You know George, just because you are not as smart, attractive or athletic as your brother, we still love you," might be a bad idea.
- If the kids are constantly bothering and fighting with each other sit them down and require them to argue for 30 minutes a day. It will make them feel really uncomfortable and they won't like it. They will stop arguing.
- When you sense jealousy, make sure to highlight what they are doing that you are proud of.
- Always make sure there is enough love and attention to go around to all of the kids. Stop and think about how you are allocating your time.
- If none of this works, embrace the opportunity. Set up a small ring in the yard and charge admission to watch the fighting, offering overpriced snacks and beverages. That is where the money is. Put the proceeds towards their college fund or for bail money.

I hope you have a great weekend!

Andy

Hello Middle School Parents!

The beautiful gems are hard to find, unless you make an effort to look. Little details in life that deserve to be acknowledged and appreciated can be so easy to overlook in a busy world. These elusive little gems that make life rich and balanced can be out of focus. Much like the needed salt in soup or ice in a cooler; when forgotten, the party of life is just not as good. This week I have been hunting gems with some success. On Tuesday, I walked into the kitchen to get a cup of coffee (that I had remembered to set up the night before. Nice!) and I just missed walking into a yellow puddle my dog left on the kitchen floor. Avoiding the agony of stepping into a mysterious liquid is reason to rejoice! On the drive to school, I made every single light. Amazing. At lunch a student lost their retainer. After about a 5-minute search through the dumpster, we found it next to a bag of discarded sliced organic peppers ($6.99 a pound out of season). For the record, over the past 16 years as a counselor, I am 9 for 11 in finding lost retainers in the dumpster...it is sort of my thing. I found a 5-dollar bill in my jacket, the clementine I ate had no seeds, I realized I did not forget trash day, and I did not have to wait in line to get my truck washed. Life is good today! The point of this is that slowing down and appreciating the small gems around us can work wonders in counteracting the negativity that surrounds us. Don't get bitten by the grumpy bunny! (My

kids get so mad when I say that.) This positivity, this no-
ticing of the small gems in life, is contagious and through
role modeling can easily be passed on to our children.

I hope you find the gems you are looking for this weekend!

Andy

• • • • • •

Hello Middle School Parents!

It harkens back to a pre-industrial time, when mother nature ruled the earth with her benevolent and omnipresent
hand. Trees, animals and plants resided in lush, dense
forests covering our land from coast to coast. The alluring
fresh smell of pine needles and cedar mixed with fallen
leaves produced a calming and reassuring scent of a place
and time that once was but still is…

Being a parent for over 18 years may have arguably
slowed the formation of my sense of self, leaving a blank
slate, eagerly ready to receive what some have coined a
"mid-life crisis." What will fill the void of "self" that has
been vacant for so long? Sports car, new job, new house,
new life, new, new, new. The answer is simple and right
under my nose. A new scent! I have never had an intentional and deliberate smell that I was aware of. Maybe all
I need is a new "signature scent." Restaurants have signature dishes and signature drinks. As a parent I am in
the service industry as well. Why can't I have a scent that
speaks to me and others? Ah, yes, the answer lies in the
"forest in a bottle." Fear not, the bottle contains goodness,
power and pride. The bottle represents the new me! At
$14.99 the Lumberjack Beard Oil is my cedar scented

round trip ticket through middle age! Way cheaper than a sports car or a new boat, beard oil will moisturize my whiskers and wash away the emptiness of me brought on by years of only thinking of not me...I have been self-promoting this new scent to my wife and kids, explaining what a big deal it really is. They are responding with lackluster confusion and annoyance. They don't seem to grasp the enormity of my new "signature scent," what I am doing or who I am becoming. Over the sounds and smells found in the lush, dense forest in my beard, I may have heard the words "weird" and "oh my gosh, get away dad" but I can't say for sure...

How different is my search for self from the struggles our middle school children are experiencing? While they may not find beard oil to be their answer, they are actively searching for who they are. The search for identity can be one of the most difficult and important challenges parents and children face. I know we have discussed this before, but below are a few additional ideas and reminders for helping your child navigate the road in their search for their identity:

- Pay attention. When your child does something that tells you about them, acknowledge it. "I noticed you dyed your hair green, you must really be excited for the game this weekend."
- Ask questions about the things they choose. Whether it is clothing, books to read or movies to watch. "I noticed you are reading 'How to deal with being a sad middle school student', is something bothering you?"
- Encourage healthy values. When your child acts in a respectful or responsible way, shows compassion or kindness, praise them and make them aware

that their behavior is noticed and appreciated. "When you chose not to kick your brother in the head after he spit on you, that showed real compassion."

- Compliment them. If they are wearing something new or have the courage to be unique, say something about it.
- Your observations and words of acknowledgement have the ability to encourage healthy and positive behavior.
- Don't be judgmental. Your style is not your kids. You don't really have style, let's be honest...
- Surround your kids with good people. If you have some friends who are knuckleheads, go to the Eagles game with them, don't bring them home.
- Continue to talk and listen to your kids. Let them talk, you listen. If they are having trouble finding their identity, they will find a way to tell you.

Give yourself a sniff this weekend. Is it time for a change?

Andy

• • • • • •

Hello Middle School Parents!

You did it again! I thought it was impossible, but you really outdid yourselves this time. Apparently, from what the kids are continuing to tell me, you have become even more annoying than anyone ever thought possible. Haven't we already spoken about this? I am told it's you that has changed, not your growing adolescent. I realize from your perspective this seems unlikely. You may feel as if your growth has only occurred in your fat stores. Perhaps when you started having children you felt a stabbing feeling, very much like when a sugar maple tree is tapped. Instead of sap slowly migrating into a metal pail, one small, sweet drip at a time, it is money, time, spontaneity and energy being slowly drained from the base of your parental trunk, making change and growth less likely. Alas, my little sugar maples, as the facts unfold, I do believe that, as surprising as this may sound, it is your child that has been undergoing some major changes that has impacted their perspective on life and on you. The main culprit here is something called autonomy.

Your child now, more than ever, has a desire for independence from a cognitive, behavioral and emotional perspective. The more we understand autonomy, the closer we may come to unraveling the mysteries and wonder of adolescent behavior. Do you remember when your kids were little, and they would always say "No?" This was the start of a desire for autonomy. Autonomy now may be hiding their cell phone or neglecting to tell you where they are going. The development and desire for autonomy is a normal healthy process that unfortunately makes you, the parent, appear to be in their eyes, the other name for a donkey, and treated as such. Below are a few reminders to think about:

- You are still reading this even though you have been referred to as a sugar maple tree and a donkey. Nice.
- Adolescents have a desire to make their own decisions.
- They often turn to others for advice and are developing the ability to see that each individual's perspective can influence the advice they give.

- Weighing the opinions and suggestions they receive, the adolescent can now come to their own decision about social, moral or ethical questions.
- Autonomy allows adolescents to manage themselves responsibly even when you are not around (most of the time).
- Middle schoolers become less emotionally dependent on their parents. They are more inclined to turn to their friends when upset, worried or need help.
- Parents are no longer viewed as "all knowing." (You are more like "know nothing," for the time being anyway.)
- Much emotional energy is invested in relationships outside of your family.
- The emotional ties are not broken with the family, they are simply changing to include others.

The next time your middle schooler questions your decision, calls you stupid, argues, seems emotionally distant, neglects to share information with you, disobeys your rules, or looks at you like you are a donkey in a sugar maple tree, take heart! The "sap" you have willingly sacrificed will one day, with a lot of continued parental effort, transform into something amazingly sweet and wonderful (or at least much better than the raw sap you have on your hands now)!

I hope you have a wonderful weekend!

Andy

· · · · · ·

Hello Middle School Parents!

The Art of War. The Art of the Steal. The Art of the Deal.

I don't want to wage war, steal things, control huge amounts of money or rip people off. I'll admit that perhaps a rush could be had by being good at these nefarious pursuits (I just had an image of riding a huge horse, wielding a broad sword, wearing a kilt with a bad comb over), but as a school counselor I have other goals.

How about this: The "Art of the Apology." Not exciting enough for you? Well hang on to your reading glasses (over 40 yet?) because I think you might be surprised! Learning how to apologize is truly an art and a powerful gateway to happiness. I have extensive experience in needing to apologize for things I did, didn't do, or did wrong. I have also noticed that middle schoolers are typically unskilled in the "Art of the Apology," which in turn leads to social turmoil that can cause havoc and unrest both at home and at school. Wouldn't life be better if they (you know who they are) said they were sorry? When I am helping children navigate the social rapids of middle school, invariably we end up discussing how to apologize. Below are a few tips and reminders to think about:

- Don't let your "but" get in the way. (Please note there is only one "t" in that word.) There is no single word that has totally messed up a good apology more than "but." "I am so sorry I hurt your feelings. That was not my intention at all. But you blah, blah, blah." Whatever you say after the "but" is the only thing the other person will hear. The "but" can be big...

- Bad hearing. It is very hard to hear what someone is saying when you are angry. It is best to deliver a meaningful apology when everyone has calmed down.
- Take ownership for your actions. When in conflict, try to step back and look in from the outside. What role did you really play in the disagreement? What could you have done differently or better? Include that in your apology.
- Listen. When the other person is talking, pay attention and try to understand their point of view.
- Swallow your pride or choke on it. Admitting you are wrong can be very difficult for people but it is a key component to resolving conflict and apologizing.
- Apologizing can prevent arguments and misunderstanding from escalating into something more. Just do it.
- The only thing harder than apologizing is being able to accept an apology. Let the anger go!
- Learn to forgive! Forgiveness is the grease that keeps the relational motor running.
- Your kids are watching. They see how you and your spouse handle apologizing. Be a good role model!
- Don't hold a grudge or the story below could happen to you...

True story: My friend's mother would cook lunch and dinner every day for her husband. The husband came home from work one day, looked at the homemade meal and said with a scowl, "What, no French fries?" The multi-layered implied message in that simple statement lit a slow burning fuse within his wife. For the next 365 days, she cooked French fries (in lard) for both lunch and dinner. Flounder, with a side of fries. Lasagna with a side of fries. Baked potatoes with a side of fries. You get the idea. Neither of them spoke about it, and he ate his fries. On the 366th day, he finally said, "are you trying to kill me?" She simply smiled at him, and lowered the basket into the hot grease, one last time...

"Making fries over this" is an expression we use in our house anytime someone is being pig headed and stubborn. Maybe you can use it too!

I hope you have a forgiving weekend, hold the fries!

Andy

• • • • • •

Hello Middle School Parents!

Every occupation has some residual impact on life outside of work. In my case, as a middle school counselor, my enjoyment of blue cheese had been compromised. Why you ask? The middle school "lost and found" can at times, smell like blue cheese. While others around me would relish in the complex and pungent flavors, to me it remained a blue veined albatross wearing an old gym uniform. My taste buds were being bamboozled. How could something be so universally loved and I, a self-proclaimed connoisseur of fine foods, find it repulsive? This culinary confusion left me feeling inadequate. Whether opting out of the blue cheese dip while eating wings or shying away from that marbled beauty on a cheese tray, the judgmental stares stabbed like blunt knives into a walnut entombed cheese log. In stout defiance to my jaded history with this nefarious cheese, I read something that provided fuel to my doggedly defiant desire to love. "Rich, buttery, piquant blue-veined cheese", read the Fearless Flyer. I confidently purchased this wedge of art, hopeful that this was indeed the cream inspired solution to my problem. I ceremoniously toasted a fresh piece of sourdough bread and anxiously encouraged the slow tide of cheese to wash across the cratered golden-brown surface. I was greeted like an old friend by a cocktail of assertive flavors that beat harmonious drums of victory on my taste buds. The missing piece to my epicurean puzzle was now firmly in place. I was free from the middle school blue cheese curse!

Your children are currently experiencing a "Blue Cheese Moment" times 100. They are confused by their bodies and their minds. They are changing and not all at the same pace. Many have retained more kid-like interests while others have started to gravitate away from such interests. The kids want to like the new but they just don't. Many are not ready. When this happens within groups of boys or girls with long histories of friendships, confusion quickly follows. Children can feel like they don't fit in. They no longer like the same things. Feelings get hurt, friendships migrate away. Making new friends, something many of our school district lifers have never had to do, can be a difficult task. Add to this the increased demands of school, all the body changes and hormone stuff, and the new cognitive abilities that make life more complicated, it is no wonder their lunch bags, hooded sweatshirts and everything else end up in the blue cheese lost and found. (Ah, ha! I was able to make this come full circle!) Forgive your children for their absent-mindedness. They have bigger cheese to cut!

The lost and found is on display in the foyer for the week. Please take note of the 26 sad lunch boxes currently without a home.

I hope you have a wonderful weekend!

Andy

March

· · · · · ·

Hello Middle School Parents!

I think it all started with the invention of wall to wall carpet. The Quaker Oats guy might have something to do
with it as well. The past two weeks I have been eating a
lot of oatmeal. My kids love eating it and the act of serving
a hot breakfast to my adolescent children makes me feel
relevant. Each morning as I pull that strangely large cyl-
inder of oats from the cabinet, I have become increasingly
intrigued by the Quaker Oats man. Have you ever *really*
looked at him? What a stew of confusion this man has cre-
ated for me. Is he kind or creepy? Benevolent grandpar-
ent or unstable scary old guy? His eyes seem to look right
through me while at the same time he seems to know
something I don't. As I stand my ground, eyes locked, my
courage starts to waiver. Does he really care about lower-
ing my cholesterol or does he have other plans for me? I

avert my gaze as I measure and dump the oats into the simmering milk (way tastier than water). I see him again on the periphery, but I don't think he sees me. Lost in a quagmire of thought, the oats seize the opportunity to angrily simmer up and over the edge of the pot with alarming speed. Did the Quaker Oats guy just laugh at me? I collect myself and refocus on my judgmental analysis of this iconic man... The powdered wig and face. This certainly gives off a privileged air. The entitled, non-calloused hand kind of soft. That's it! There could be a lesson buried within the oats! Is your child in danger of turning into the soft Quaker Oats man while lounging in the wall to wall carpet luxury of life?

As parents, we often strive to do so much for our children. We want "the best" for our kids and will make incredible sacrifices to reach this end. We have worked to create a home and life for our children that could, perhaps, run the risk of making them soft – too soft. Ultimate comfort and ease of living seems to be associated with suburban success and being a good parent. What good ever came from easy? "Easy" does not help in the formation of pride, self-worth, accountability, work ethic, and appreciation. How can we as parents help encourage these traits that are arguably the foundation for resiliency? Below are a few ideas (some of which will sound crazy) that you can do at home to prevent your child from turning into the Quaker Oats man:

- Chores. Just playing sports and going to school is not enough. Sports are supposed to be a fun activity. A luxury if you will. The house still needs to be cleaned, the garbage taken out, etc. Doing chores is a good thing.

- Camping. Heat, indoor plumbing, electricity. These things are awesome and totally taken for granted by so many. Take your kids camping and live without for a little while. No toilet? You don't know what you've got till it's gone...

- Embrace power outages. Light the fireplace, candles and put on some extra clothes. (Don't turn on the generator until you see a cold blue tinge on the surface of your child's skin.)

- Turn down the water heater. What if, (this is a big what if) there was only enough hot water for everyone to take a short shower in the morning? Working together, thinking about the "other guy," being considerate. All of this could, in theory, be derived from less hot water.

- A *little* pain is good. It can be excruciating to see your child struggle in school, sports, etc. Our first instinct is to step in and help resolve the problem. Giving our children some time to find a solution on their own is a proven pathway to growth.

- Do it yourself. A few years ago, we got some mulch delivered. The wife of a very good friend said in all seriousness, "Wow, I didn't know that was something you could do yourself." Have your kids involved in the annual home projects, such as mulch, leaf clean up, etc. They live there too.

- Heat. Would the kids turn the heat up if that meant bringing in firewood and getting up at 4 am to light the wood stove? Would they leave the front door open? While heating with wood is certainly not for everyone, it can help children to understand and value what it takes to warm a home. (At a minimum, explain the energy bill to them.)

- Shared sacrifice. Save money together as a family and set a goal. Pay up. Save up. Have them earn it.

I hope you have a wonderful, tough, oat inspired weekend!

Andy

• • • • • •

Shared experiences

Hello Middle School Parents!

Let's talk briefly about shared experiences. Take a moment and think about your closest friends in life. Now, break it down. Are you thinking about the people or the experiences and memories you have shared with these people? It is the shared experiences we have in life that bring us together. The most powerful experiences are often connected with hard work, reaching a goal or simply going through something together that was challenging. These experiences could fall into the category of "shared sacrifice." Running a marathon with a friend, breaking down while driving across country, making it through military boot camp, having children, building a log cabin in the woods with your hippy college roommate. You get the idea. These real-life experiences act as the glue that keeps you connected with your friends many years later. Why not apply this same idea to your family? Create shared experiences as a family unit. How can you do this? Include everyone! As a family, what goals do you have? What are you interested in? What projects are you working on? Your children are getting older, stronger, smarter and they are ready and willing to contribute and become a more active member of your family team. Here are some ideas that might get you started:

- Planning a family vacation? Start a fund to pay for it. Have the children come up with some ways to make money so they can contribute too. (My kids have helped bank roll my annual trip to Vegas for the past 5 years... I keep forgetting to bring them!)
- Do you have any projects around the house that you are planning on doing yourself? Have your children help you with it. They are way more capable than they were just a few years ago. Be patient, teach them how to do it. Accept less than perfect work as long as they are trying. (Have them practice any major home improvements on your mother-in-law's house before your own, just to work the kinks out.)
- Even the small day to day tasks are best done together. Mini accomplishments can add up. Cooking dinner, doing the dishes together, making lunches, folding laundry. I know, exciting stuff but still capable of producing a memory and still something they can take pride in.
- Read a book together as a family. This summer take 20 minutes every night to read aloud to your children. Pick a book that you all can enjoy. Slow down, technology off, go old school and take the time. You will be surprised how much your children will all enjoy this. It will give you all something to talk about. A common connection.
- Traveling in the car? Listen to a book on tape together. It is much easier to let each kid get consumed into their own piece of technology but fight the power! Have a discussion, pick a book and make it happen.

- Go for a hike together. Geocaching is very fun to keep everyone interested. (Look it up to learn more if you are not familiar with it.)
- Create your own Survivor game! Go camping deep in the woods, in the spring, when the bears are coming out of hibernation. Neglect to bring food, water, shelter or any fire making tools. Plan on staying out 10 days. If you make it home, you will all have a shared experience to last a lifetime!

When children have to work for things in life, they value and appreciate them more. Children might complain and give you all kinds of grief about their involvement. Expect this. Know that if you are consistent, they will learn that their family contribution and involvement is not only expected, but valued, appreciated and fun! Most importantly, the shared experiences you create with your family will bring you all closer. These will be childhood memories they have forever. "Remember when dad would make us build and paint all of the custom recycling bins he loved so much?" As a bonus, your child may think twice about throwing a lacrosse ball against the garage door if last year he spent 4 hours (with you), scraping, sanding and painting it!

I hope you have a great weekend!

Andy

• • • • • •

Mood swings

Hello Middle School Parents!

The old Victorian home sits proudly near the water, boasting a beautiful covered porch with a tongue and groove pine ceiling painted a calming robin's egg blue. One cascading hanging flower basket after another are graciously holding hands. The ginger bread moldings are meticulously maintained and loved in a cacophony of inspired color. The railings are waist high, with cutout sailboats happily replacing the traditional spindles. A pleasantly cool and gentle prevailing wind is carrying the smells of cedar and fresh water. There are no cedar trees, so there must be a handsome man in a boat nearby wearing beard oil… It is 68 degrees with low humidity. No need for Gold Bond Powder. No sweating today my friend. The sun dominates the sky, dancing in practiced harmony with the shy cirrus clouds. There you sit, on a hand-crafted porch swing, fresh mint infused drink in hand, laughing and talking with old friends. What day of the week is it? Where are the kids? The slow and intentional back and forth of the swing is the final touch to a perfect, relaxing afternoon. You conclude that indeed, swings are amazing, until you get home…

Upon your return to reality, you are greeted by your adolescent child, who is eager to share another type of swing with you known as "mood swings." Ahh! What has happened to your idyllic setting and wonderful child? Over the past two weeks I have received numerous calls from parents asking if their child's behavior is "normal." Their children have started to act crazy and they are concerned. Below are a few tips and reminders for managing this inevitable, and not normally pleasant part of parenting:

- Leave them alone. When your kid is acting crazy, that is not the time to try and talk logically with them. Mood swings are like the flu. There is no known cure for mood swings but parental vaccinations are available daily at the Berwyn Tavern.

- Keep the rats away. When your child is experiencing mood swings keep your other kids away. Siblings are drawn to emotional weakness like a jubilant Eagles fan to a greased light post.

- Swings go both ways. When your child is feeling great, that is the time to talk with them about how they have been feeling and the best ways to manage those feelings.

- Put them to bed. Well rested children will have less frequent and shorter mood swings. You should get some sleep too. You are way nicer when well rested...

- Don't take the bait. Sometimes moody adolescents will say things specifically so you will lose your cool.

- Take lessons from the WWF. The World Wrestling Federation has been responsible for many a good parenting tip. Tony Atlas and Rocky Johnson in 1983 mastered the art of the tag out. When you are on the mat, in an emotional figure four leg lock, about to lose the parenting match to your adolescent, tag your partner and take a break. Know when to walk away, know when to run...

- Love and attention. Keep showing and expressing your love even when they don't deserve it.

- Good food and exercise can lessen the severity of mood swings. Calmly sauté some nice greens with tilapia and a side of quinoa while your kid is yelling at you and serve it up with a smile!

- Remember that this is temporary and yes, mood swings are totally normal.

Good times are right around the corner. Your seat on the porch swing will be there waiting for you!

Andy

• • • • • •

Hello Middle School Parents!

The story ended with the dog throwing up on her bed. He had apparently eaten copious amounts of grass and what appeared to be pieces of a tennis ball... Sorry, I am getting ahead of myself. Susie was talking with me about how difficult it was for her to complete her homework. She just did not have enough time! When Susie gets home from school at 3:15, she eats a snack and then takes her dog for a walk. She also plays field hockey, but that is in the fall. On Monday, Wednesday and Friday she has swimming lessons until 7:00 and on Tuesday she has piano lessons. When she gets back home, typically she will eat dinner, shower and get to her homework. She works in her room and takes an "occasional" break, diving into the worm hole of social media. Maybe a quick show on Netflix ("Mom, have you ever seen the show Friends? It's awesome!") and then back to Algebra. Susie really needs her phone to do her homework. The next thing she knows, it is 11:00 at night. She closes the books and puts her phone next to her bed. Leave the phone down stairs you suggest? It is her alarm clock too! How will she ever get up on time without it? (Someone should invent a clock that makes noise at the time you tell it to so you wake up.) Almost asleep... is that Robert snap chatting me... up again. She finally falls asleep and the dog barfs on her

103

bed, chunky style, my favorite. School is going to be tough in the morning.

How can you help your inefficient adolescent learn to manage their time in the challenging middle school world? The kids have more responsibilities and activities than ever. The school work has increased and simply memorizing is not going to cut it. Doing the minimum to "get it done" is not going to work. They need to actually learn it. Being a real student takes time. Below are a few reminders and ideas that you can discuss with your child that might be helpful in finding a balance:

- How are they using their study hall time at school? Most kids have one a few times a week. A solid 45 minutes of time to get their homework completed and get help from their teachers. They can also discreetly make paper footballs, go to the bathroom and fall asleep with their eyes open.
- Is there a productive routine after school? Having a schedule or routine to follow after school can help avoid the time traps. Writing down an hour by hour daily schedule can help.
- What are the time traps? Ask your child to identify the ways they waste time. Simply being aware of what these are can help. Insider tip: when I unofficially asked the kids, Netflix was number one on the list. When we were kids, the huge boxy blaring TV made it obvious we were watching Fantasy Island at 10:30 at night. Today, the kids sneak it. Does your child ever "go to the bathroom" and 45 minutes later they emerge? More fiber needed? Probably not. Check your movie watching account. You might be able to see how much they watch.

- Driving to activities that are far away? It might be possible to do work in the car. Audio books, review notes, etc. This can be productive time when needed.
- Stay organized. Ask your child to show you their "system" for organization. If it looks a mess, try to help. When they tell you that you are stupid and to get out of their room, call your school counselor for help!
- What areas are truly difficult? Is it the math homework or studying for social studies tests? If you can help your child identify the problem areas, and really break it down, it is easier to trouble shoot. There are resources at school to help with any problem! Ask your child to be an advocate for themselves and to come in and talk with their counselor.

Just today, my 9th grader was up at 4:30 a.m. to finish his homework. He only had about 7 waking hours to complete it after school yesterday… I think I may have to try some of these ideas!

Andy

• • • • • •

Friendships

Hello Middle School Parents!

It is amazing how important friends are to middle school students! I am convinced that school and the work associated with it, to many adolescents, is simply an inconvenience they must deal with in order to hang out with their friends. Just this week I was doing my best sell job to a 5th grader on the importance of homework and efficient study habits when I realized she was not listening at all! What was she really thinking about? In an effort not to breach confidentiality, I will tell you that her best friend likes the same boy she does, but the boy doesn't know it! When they saw him walking down the hall, they hid in the art room. OMG, I know! Crazy! Have I shared too much?

To adults, the trials and tribulations associated with the social maneuverings, so deftly and clumsily executed by adolescents, can seem trivial, insignificant, and frustrating. To our children, making and keeping friends is their number one priority. Have you ever found yourself saying things like "if you just went in for extra help and got a few more points, your B+ would be an A." Have you ever seen a child spend hours on a homework assignment or project only to forget to turn it in? These things happen because school is a few notches down on the priority list. School is simply not what they are thinking about. Yes, doing well in school is really important, however, supporting positive friendships can and will benefit your child in many different areas. Friends can and should take up a lot of time. Here are some things to think about:

- Having friends is critical to their social development. It helps them develop emotionally. By interacting with friends, they learn social skills, communication and problem-solving skills.
- Kids with good friends are healthier, do better in school and don't get bullied as much.
- Friends can minimize the negative impact of family problems.
- Friends can make kids less anxious about trying new things.
- Friends can validate kids in a way that means more than their parents' words ever can. Kids know that

parents love them but someone, like a friend, shows them affection who doesn't have to, it has a stronger impact.

- Teens develop social skills by hanging out with their peers. How to meet people, converse in small groups, make small talk, be teased and gently tease back and generally share funny stories and jokes is one of the most important parts of friendship.
- If you are a good friend your child will be too! Remember, they are always watching!
- Get to know your child's friends. Offer to drive them places. Talk with their friends while they are in the car. You will learn a lot!
- Try to get to know the parents. You don't have to be best friends with them but learn enough to make sure they have similar rules and values. What their philosophies are on parenting, supervision, etc.

Even though it can be exhausting as a parent to watch the social ups and downs, it is all part of the middle school challenge! Navigating the rough social terrain is not easy but it is critical to their development as a person. If your child is having any difficulties with balancing school and friends, talk to your counselor!

I hope you have a great weekend!

Andy

· · · · · ·

Hello Middle School Parents!

"Push it! Push it real good!" I believe these seemingly spicy lyrics from Salt-N-Peppa in 1987 were actually intended to be a source of inspiration for adolescents around the globe. Both Salt and Peppa were clearly at the forefront of the positive parent movement. This catchy and rhythmic tune talking about the boundaries your adolescent child is currently pushing continues to inspire...

Many of the parents I have spoken to this week have verified the kids are pushing the boundaries "real good" indeed. Perhaps you weren't ready for this? Did it sneak up on you like old age or unwanted body hair? When your child is pushing the boundaries, it can be more frustrating than a roving maintenance crew on the highway...

When you had a baby, it was very clear you needed to "baby proof" your house. Cushioned corners, cabinet locks, covers on all of the electrical outlets and always a watchful eye for anything that could be a choking hazard. After years of vigilance, parents become permanently hardwired to ensure the safety of their children. To this day my one teenager will put plastic wrap over his mouth and both his mother and grandmother scream for him to stop, fearing he will suffocate. He laughs. I laughed the first time he did it, which was not well received... Are his antics sick or funny? Both maybe. Perhaps neither? Either way, you now have another job as a parent; You need to prepare your house yet again by creating safe and effective boundaries for your middle school child to live and grow within. Below are a few tips and reminders for setting effective and appropriate boundaries that will hopefully help you to keep your sanity:

- It is normal for kids to push the limits to see where they stand. This is a normal part of forming their identity and developing their own set of beliefs and values.
- Let's say your kid cheats on a test. They are totally guilty and you know it. Do you bail your kid out by calling the teacher or support the natural consequences, encouraging resilience and problem-solving skills? They need to understand the consequences of their choices. Don't bail them out! (If they are actually in jail you should bail them out. Jail sounds scary. That was just an expression.)
- Set your boundaries for what you expect of your child. Be consistent and firm. The second you start making exceptions, they sense the weakness. Dog on the couch? Let it sleep there once and you are done! Be consistent!
- They are supposed to question authority. This is normal and developmentally appropriate and part of their search for an identity.
- Spend a lot of time explaining what you expect of your child. Be very clear and specific about expectations and rules. The more immature they are, the more time you will need to spend explaining.
- Tell your child you love them, even when they are driving you crazy!!!

hope you have a wonderful weekend!

Andy

· · · · · ·

Hello Middle School Parents!

It hurts. It really, really hurts. My wife tells me my tolerance for pain is embarrassingly low. She is very skilled and direct in communicating this to me whenever I injure myself. This time though, seriously, it hurt. I was engaged in one of the many manly activities I partake in each and every day, when something went terribly wrong. I was chain sawing large logs, picking up the rounds (pieces of wood to you non-lumberjacks) and tossing them aside. (I think the scene looked very much like an old Genesee Cream Ale commercial – the great outdoors in a can – but I can't be sure). As I picked up a meager 12-inch piece of red oak, I felt and heard a loud popping noise from my lower back. I am not a doctor and I don't play one on TV, but my assumption that this was bad turned out to be accurate. Ending up on the wood floor at 1:30 in the morning, unable to walk, and having time to think, I concluded that back pain and raising middle school children have a few things in common:

- Children and sprained sacroiliac (SI) joints both have the capacity to cause great pain.
- At the worst, most painful parenting and back pain moments, it is easy to feel like things will never get better.
- Both respond well to consistent gentle heat (parental pressure/moist heat) when necessary.
- Adolescents and sprained SI joints will both improve over time. (7- 10 days for the SI joint. Can be years for your kid. You have to believe!)
- You are stuck with both your child and your spine, so you had better take care of them.

110

- Complaining to your spouse about either of them is a waste of time.
- When you ask too much from either your kid or your back, that is when things start to hurt!

I hope you have a great weekend!

Andy

April

Hello Middle School Parents!

I just can't stop myself from taking more! I know I shouldn't, but I do. Time and time again my ineffective morally infused self-talk fails to curtail my habit. Can you blame me? They sit neatly in a plastic cup on the counter, beautiful in their uniform appearance; Orderly, clean, utilitarian, and most of all, tantalizingly free! Sure, they give me a couple, but if I ask for, or simply take more, nobody seems to mind. A guilty pleasure or a mild disorder? Call it what you will, but I really like the free paint stirring sticks from the paint counter at the hardware store...

The allure of "free" can be powerful especially when newly discovered. I have great news for you! There is something gloriously free right in front of your eyes that is good for everyone involved. Some may judgingly refer to this as "child labor." I, however, believe getting your child off their butt to help with chores and jobs around the house can be amazing! Lets' take a closer look.

Your kids are older now and on their way to growing up. They are at the precipice of wanting to remain a child while at the same time longing to be treated as a young adult. As parents, if we can find moments to recognize this new little adult as a contributing member of the household it can work wonders for their self-esteem and self-worth. Just the other day I asked a student how their weekend was. He told me his weekend was great and that he helped his mom paint the hallway. He felt proud. Proud that he was asked to help and proud that he was able to do a decent job. A total win!

Here are a few tips to getting your free workforce up and running:

- Figure out the ability level of your child and then bump it a little higher. Challenge them to rise to the occasion. Painting the fence sounds great! Climbing the extension ladder to paint the second floor, maybe not. That could be a job for your mother-in-law.
- Accept less than perfect work, they are in middle school!
- Have a discussion with them about all the chores you do each day. Find out which ones they would be willing to do and give them a chance to get into the routine. Show them how you want it done.
- Don't assume. Your son may love to help you with sewing the curtains and your daughter may totally enjoy learning how the drill press works. Invite their participation and let them decide.

- Be patient! Don't lose your cool if they mess up. They will mess up and that's OK.
- Could you do it faster on your own? Maybe. Slow down and allot more time for the job so you don't feel rushed.
- By involving your child in your chores/hobbies/projects, they might stumble upon something they are really good at. Learning what they enjoy and what they are good at is one of the major goals of middle school.

I hope you have a wonderful weekend!!

Andy

• • • • • •

Hello Middle School Parents!

Have you ever thrown a Saltine at a chicken? My first time was this past Sunday, and my life will never be the same. I was sitting next to our fire pit in the back yard eating Saltines and enjoying life. The dog came over (we spend a lot of time together now that we have the electric fence) and he tried to eat the small pile of crackers that were "on deck" waiting to be enjoyed. I intervened, but not before he prodded the pile with his slobbery loose jowls and wet nose. In an effort to preserve the mood, I was going to ignore this infraction and continue eating them. My wife said something along the lines of "you are a pig" which, after 20 years of marriage I quickly translated to "don't eat the crackers." Then something special happened. The deeply buried undiscovered Irish warrior bubbled to the surface and the landscape morphed into a bat-

114

efield. Out of the corner of my eye I saw one of our chick-
ns pecking on the ground about 10 feet from my
hair. Picking up a Saltine as a Ninja might wield a
hrowing star, in a skilled and fluid movement, I launched
hat small salty beacon of high blood pressure, hitting the
hicken squarely on what I think might be the drum stick
egion of the bird. The Irish Warrior left as soon as he
ppeared and my cognizant disbelief at performing this
nprecedented feat, manifested itself in pure jubilation. I
prung from my deep-seated chair yelling something like,
Did you see that? I hit the chicken with the Saltine!" To
ay disappointment and surprise, my wife and children
ailed to see the enormity of what I had just accomplished,
ach displaying a disinterested, unimpressed, and
trangely concerned countenance…alas, greatness is so of-
en hard to see by the masses.

he chickens, while being excellent targets for harmless
nack foods, have also provided our family with many val-
able lessons over the years. Patience, slowing down,
hores, family time, family activities and projects. Many
f the things we have discussed this year about parenting
niddle schoolers are part of the "chicken experi-
nce." Let's take a closer look:

- Back to basic chicken chores are healthy, old fash-
  ioned and good for kids. (Telling the kids to go clean
  out the chicken coop when I am upset with them is
  highly gratifying.)
- Death. Everyone and everything loves to eat
  chicken. Early on we would name the chickens and
  soon realized this made their inevitable demise
  that much harder. The chickens are free range and
  with that privilege comes risk (hawks, raccoons,
  fox, etc.) Our kids learned the cycle of life and

death because of the chickens. They are not insen sitive but rather have some experience and an un derstanding of it.

- Building the hen house itself was a fun family chore. I "borrowed" the old Snoopy House that was used for a middle school play years ago and we con verted it.

- The whole "farm to table" movement can't get any closer to home than when you eat eggs from your own chickens. Our children understand a little more about where food actually comes from and they still get enjoyment from going to get the eggs

- Chickens eat ticks and bugs in the backyard. (If your kids ever get lice you can buy a "chicken hat" that allows 1 chicken to free range on your kids head and eat all of the lice…)

- They eat many kinds of food scraps that would oth erwise end up in the trash or garbage disposal.

- Caring for the young chicks is a family affair as well, requiring consistency, attention and patience that is often lost on kids today.

- The chicken manure when composted is amazing on the garden. (The chore of bringing things to the compost bin is another good activity for adoles cents.)

- Watching chickens is relaxing, simple, and makes you slow down. It may also allow your ancestral roots a chance to emerge again, if only for a brief incredible moment, that perhaps only you will truly understand.

*This message was jointly funded by the Council for Chicken Ownership and Saltines, "the cracker that packs a punch."

I hope you have a wonderful weekend!

Andy

· · · · · ·

Hello Middle School Parents!

For the past 16 years, I have been asking my wife if I could please go away for spring break. Cancun, South Padre Island, Fort Lauderdale, it really does not matter. My motivation and altruistic goal is to allow my wife quality, independent time with the children...and alas, every single year she patiently and calmly tells me, "No." She will then outline alternative plans that will be "even more fun." This year I am scrubbing out our recycling bins and changing out the ignitors on our grill. Few things in life are as satisfying as throwing an empty can of tuna fish into a brilliantly clean bin. And that swoosh sound when the grill lights on the first push of the button is simply magical...

Some students have told me they are going away for the break and many are staying home. Here are a few ideas of fun things to do with your family in the event you are not stealing away to a chalet in the heart of France or perhaps chartering a yacht through the Canary Islands:

- Visit Delaware! The kids will be overjoyed knowing it is the "first state."
- Take out their school papers from the first half of the year and play a fun review game.
- Make a few treasure maps of your yard and encourage the kids to dig holes. When they are done,

plant some spring flowers in those very same holes.

- Take the kids dirt sledding. During the next rain, head out to your local park and attempt to make your way down a large hill. When the park rangers take notice of you, tell the kids the game is now called hide and seek. (Misdemeanors are not that big of a deal.)
- Go fishing in a local river. The recent dumping of 250,000 gallons of sewage encourages the fish to float which makes them easier to catch.
- Alert! An Alberta Clipper confluence coupled with a cold-air-funnel will combine with Artic air this weekend. I think that means it might snow. Have a family snow shoveling contest and the losers clean out the recycling bins.

I hope you have a great Spring Break!! Relax, laugh and have fun with your family!

Andy

• • • • • •

Hello Middle School Parents!

The long-awaited sounds coming from the trees and sky were mesmerizing, purposeful and reassuring. It had been a long winter and the birds were welcoming in spring with open arms. Like a shy child in a beautiful dress, the flowers had finally mustered up the courage to reveal themselves. The air was crisp linen clean, washed, and refreshing. I walked slowly into the school building, relishing the newness of spring and the wonderful and anticipated changes that were taking place all around me. Little did

I know that I would soon be reminded it is more than the miracle of spring that is undergoing changes...

Abruptly at 9:05 that day, the nurse came running into my office. A student had fainted. We rushed down the hallway together, awkwardly pushing the empty wheel chair through a maze of gawking children. Arriving at room 115, it was the absolute eerie silence that struck me first, then the hushed darkness. There was indirect light, guilty light, coming from the overhead projector, daring me to look. I was astonished. There before me was a larger than life (in most cases anyway) projection of anatomically correct, labeled, male and female body parts. This was 7th grade health class. The year was 2005. The unsuspecting victim of truth was passed out on the floor next to his desk. The reality of how this stuff all worked had apparently overwhelmed him. You do what with what? Seriously? The nurse deftly helped the boy up off the tile floor and into the wheel chair. The confusing facts of life hung heavily in the air, as I took in this true middle school moment.

Ok, let's get to it. Have you done it? Have you had those potentially super awkward talks with your kid about the birds and the bees? Have you had the talks that could prevent your child from passing out on their honeymoon? Below are a few tips and reminders for dealing with this often difficult task:

- If you don't teach your kids about sex, someone else will. The older kids on the bus, their peers or scarily, the internet.
- If they have seen inappropriate things on the internet, it is important to explain that that is not real life and most people do not act that way. Exposure

to pornography on the internet is one of the biggest differences between now and when we grew up.

- They learn the nuts (no pun here) and bolts of the human body in health. The anatomy, the diseases, etc. You as the parent need to put all of this in the right moral context based on your beliefs and values. What does a relationship mean? How should people treat each other, etc.

- No matter how awkward it may seem, and the kids will never admit it, they do want to talk with you, their parents, about this.

- Talking to your kids about sex does not ruin their innocence.

- This is not a one and done conversation. Having many ongoing conversations over the years is best.

- Driving in the car or taking a walk are good times for such heavy conversation. It is easier to talk about delicate subjects when you don't have to make eye contact. Don't be weird about it. If every time you get in the car you talk about sex, they are going to start calling an Uber.

- Don't make up stuff. If you don't know the answer to a question your kids ask, get back to them after you have the correct information.

- Talk about puberty before you talk about sex.

- If your kids are asking you questions and talking about this, you have already established an open, inviting, and caring atmosphere. Good job!

- If your child does ask questions, you can use that to figure out the sources of their information. "Great question. What made you think to ask that?"

- There is way more to this, but I hope this can at least get you started!

hope you have a wonderful weekend talking about sex!

Andy

• • • • • •

Hello Middle School Parents!

To this day, I will never admit it to him. For many years I have implemented an unsuccessful strategy of sustained denial in hopes that it becomes "the truth." His mind is sharp. He knows the real truth, as do I. I am not proud of what I did, but at the time, I could not help myself.

Growing up, my older brother and I would play a lot of games together. To my dismay and frustration, he would win the majority of the time.   Computer games on our Apple IIe, Atari and the classic board games were all tools he masterfully used for the good natured, emotional and mo-ale depleting beatings he would bestow upon me. In his classic, high handed way, another Monopoly deal had been truck leaving him with the purples and the goldfish col-ored properties and I with the utilities and the greens. Having the greens is useless without a lot of money, of which I had little. One hour later the game ab-ruptly ended. The Chance card directed me to his hotel on St. Charles Place, with me "supposedly" throwing the board game into the air, crying, running out of the room…

Parenting is very much like Monopoly. Community Chest and Chance cards. The phone call from school. The report from the doctor. The e-mail from the coach. You can never tell what is going to happen. Things could be going really well, and then the cards. Maybe something good happens, maybe not. $10 for the second place in the beauty contest or your kid is failing math. The parental anxiety comes from the unknown, the things out of your control. You just built and then bam! You get the Houses and Hotels repair card. Up and down it goes. Having children is, in part, a game of the unknown, a game of worry and a game of love. You have to prepare and hope that when you pull the "Advance to Boardwalk" card there is not a hotel waiting for you. Perhaps you have a $500 bill under the board? I hope so. The older your children get, the more adult like their problems become. The older your children get, the more accumulated time and energy they have invested into their school work, sports, activities and life in general. The stakes are higher. The more invested, the more risk taken. A friend just the other day told me, "you are only as happy as your saddest kid." So true. As parents, how can we support our children when the game of life is not going their way?

Below are a few tips and reminders for supporting our children when they are faced with serious adversity or setbacks:

- Stay positive. There is good to be had from any situation if you look for it.
- Avoid focusing on what you lost, instead, highlight what you still have.
- Call in a solid. There are many people who positively influence your children. Counselors, teachers, coaches, friends, relatives. Enlist their help.
- It is OK to grieve. When something bad happens, it is often a loss of some kind. Allow some time to be sad.
- Believe in your child. You have done all of the tough prep work getting your child ready for

- life. Trust that they will overcome the problem or setback.
- Circle the wagons. When dealing with real problems, enlisting the help and empathy of your immediate family is crucial. Your family is a team. You win and lose together.
- Step up. Your child will need your support now more than ever. Thinking logically is difficult when highly emotional. They may need you to do some of the thinking and planning for them.
- Listen to them. When they want to talk, make the time to listen.
- Tell your child you love them, you are proud of them, and reassure them and yourself that everything will be OK.

I hope you have a wonderful weekend! A game of Monopoly anyone?

Andy

• • • • • •

Quality time

Hello Middle School Parents!

"Hot dogs can bring a family together." Have you ever heard that slogan? Perhaps it is new to you because I just made it up. You might be skeptical in this assertion that a highly processed meat product can strengthen family bonds. It does sound ridiculous to argue that a tube of extruded animal parts could be the glue that holds the family together, but I have proof. One of our friends (in her 30s at the time) was invited by her father to go to lunch. She was happy to receive the invitation, got coverage for her young children and made all of the other necessary preparations for a nice afternoon out with her father. Nectar, The White Dog Cafe or perhaps the Capital Grill? She was excited for a special lunch! He picked her up and they proceeded to drive to The Home Depot. "Dad, do you need to pick something up before lunch? Why are we at the Home Depot?" He looked at her in a confused way and said "No honey, we are having lunch here. These are the best hot dogs around!" They had a wonderful lunch together, talking, and laughing while admiring the various grills and fencing products in the front of the store.

Just this week, and I am not sure why, three different 8th grade girls mentioned to me that their fathers loved taking them to The Home Depot for hot dogs! While they all found it funny, they all admitted to enjoying this time with their dads. They also raved about the hot dogs while showing indifference to the various styles of fencing.

Spending time with your kids and sharing with them the things you enjoy is a good idea for old and young parents alike!

I hope you have a wonderful processed meat filled weekend!

Andy

• • • • • •

Get outside

Hello Middle School Parents!

It was one of the best moments of my life. My resourcefulness, strength, and greatness had never shined so brightly. This memory, this historic and epic tale has been, and will continue to be, passed down from generation to generation until the end of time. The year was 1983, and it was most certainly a different time. Living in a neighborhood full of kids, under-scheduled and free to roam, we played. Yes, we did play video games, but Pit Fall, Adventure and Asteroids can only hold one's attention for so long. The inevitable suburban "call of the almost wild" would ring in our ears, luring us all outside. Tackle football in the neighbor's yard, racing matchbox cars down the chaise lounges or burning anything that moved with a magnifying glass all provided solid entertainment, but the main attraction was something bigger. A warm summer night, 14 middle school boys, and parents unburdened with the worries of today allowed it all to happened. Manhunt. Have you ever played? It is a glorified game of hide and seek mixed with tag. There is a jail for those captured. Our boundaries were the entire neighborhood, including every yard, even the people we did not know. Executing a jailbreak, freeing your teammates, required skill, patience, courage and a little luck. The luck part was Russel. A nice kid plagued with being confusingly slow at running. Intelligent and kind, but slow. Really slow. Russel was in hot pursuit as I ran down the middle of the road to the dead end. Having only a few minutes to act, I pulled out my lighter and lit two smoke bombs (I did tell you it was a different time.) The beautiful blue and red smoke melding into a welcomed purple haze. A hiding, concealing haze, that Russel ran straight into. Temporarily stunned that the smoke bombs were actually working as planned, I refocused on my mission, rolling under a nearby car, "vanishing." In a dumbfounded, smoke induced stupor, Russel errantly ran off in pursuit of his prize that was laying under the sporty yet practical Buick Skylark. With Russel the jailkeeper hood-winked, I successfully freed my teammates, forever more becoming a Manhunt legend…

Spring is here! Get your kids outside!! It might seem like your kids have not been out of the house in a "Fortnite"…

Below are a few ideas, tips and reminders for helping your child to have fun outside and maybe, just maybe, become a legend in their own mind too:

• Go Fishing! Teaching your child to fish is a life - long skill. Taking a weekend to go fishing can be a wonderful bonding experience. Consider spicing it up a bit by not bringing food. If you have to catch your dinner or go hungry, this can be very motiva-tional…

• Camping. This can be amazing. Borrow supplies from a friend if you don't have the right equip-ment. If you don't know what you are doing, get that friend to go with you. If things don't go well like rain, mosquitos, or sharing your dinner with a black bear, it is guaranteed to be a lasting family memory.

• Buy your kid a magnifying glass and teach them how to use it. Looking and learning about insects close up is cool. Burning things is cool too…

• Birds. Point out the birds, especially on a spring morning. Our area is flush with beautiful birds. This is a good time to remind you that when they act disinterested they are still listening to what you are saying. I think so anyway. You have to believe.

126

- Teach your child about the stars. If there is some kind of extra special event going on like a comet, bringing the family outside to see it is fun.
- Grow legal plants. Planting a small garden or even flower boxes is a wonderful family project.
- Laser tag in the backyard is really fun. The equipment can be a little expensive, but it is a good time. You can sit back next to the firepit and watch the kids run around.
- I looked out my back widow the other night and saw Cars 2 playing on my neighbor's garage door. Outdoor projectors appear to be a good compromise for kids who don't like being outside.
- Leave them alone. If the kids are outside playing, let them engage their imagination. They don't always need organized or planned activities.

hope you have a wonderful weekend outside in this warm weather we are having!!!

Andy

MAY

· · · · · ·

Hello Middle School Parents!

Tutu 2, Gramzy, Nana375, memom4. These were some of the license plates I saw as I walked through the middle school parking lot on my way to my daughter's lacrosse game. Approaching the baseball field, I saw a small gaggle of grandparents carrying their folding chairs, slowly making their way to the sidelines. I was able to hear their conversations, a compilation of scenes from Grumpy Old Men and Cocoon. Mary had just purchased new cleats for her granddaughter, her husband, who was not listening, was talking to his son about something he saw on Fox News. Francine had been there for over an hour because she got the time of the game wrong. General agreement was made regarding how heavy many of these folding camping chairs were. One person was even talking about their new recycling bins (I think that was my dad). It is awesome that so many grandparents are able to attend

128

their grandchildren's games! Being around our parents, at times, can make us feel embarrassed: "you can't say things like that," grateful: "thank you for helping with the kids," burdened: "I can carry your chair," happy: "I loved watching you and John fishing together," frustrated: "I told you the game was at 9," worried: "the person who called is not really going to fix your computer." Pick any of these emotions and the answer could be yes! If you are lucky enough to still have your parents around and even luckier if they are positively involved in the lives of your own children, here are a few reminders and ideas for keeping the relationships strong:

- Besides you, nobody loves your kids more than their grandparents.
- Adolescents with involved grandparents are better at bouncing back from setbacks.
- Having healthy connections with other adults (like grandparents) can be one of the most important factors in teens developing into successful adults.
- Grandparents can be amazing help with watching the kids and even paying for stuff! Want to increase the odds? If they are taking your kid out to dinner, make them wear a pair of shoes with holes in them or a coat on that is too small. They might come home with something new and nice!
- Remember, they want the best for your children and they do have experience raising kids. (You turned out OK. Well, sort of.)
- Be on the same page with your spouse about how you want to raise your kids. When grandparents cross the line of what you think is acceptable, you need to talk with them about it. This is more effective than letting your annoyance simmer and stew.

- If your parents are opinionated, try not to get angry. Smile and say something like "thank you for your suggestion that we give Buddy 12 ounces of Brandy for his cold. We will think about it."
- If things get really bad, leave informational booklets on the kitchen counter from disreputable, chronically out of compliance, low-end, senior living facilities located in high crime areas...

I hope you enjoy your family and have fun this weekend!

Andy

• • • • • •

Hello Middle School Parents!

When I was in graduate school at Villanova (I think I was recruited to play basketball, but I can't remember) I had a professor named Nick Rosa. He explained that when counseling people, it is often like a circular river. A client will say something significant and if you miss the opportunity to encourage their further exploration of the topic, there is no need to worry. If it is important to the client, that topic will come back around, very much like a raft floating in a circular river. I tell you this because I feel this analogy applies to parenting middle school children and can impact your perspective as you watch them struggle to form their own identity.

Two years ago, my son wanted to learn to play the guitar. We proceeded to buy a guitar and drive him to lessons every week. As the year progressed his interest waned and attending the lessons became a battle. He eventually stopped playing. After putting time and money into this endeavor, I was annoyed and suggested to my wife that we sell the **** guitar. She told me to calm down and go clean out the recycling bins. Two years after that first lesson, I noticed the guitar resting in the stand in the corner of the living room. My wife put it there as "bait," just to see what might happen. This past week, I heard music coming from upstairs. My son was learning to play a song by watching a video on You Tube. I instantly thought of this guitar floating around a circular river. I also patted myself on the back for marrying someone smarter than myself.

My take away from this, from a parenting perspective, is patience! Middle school children are evolving, changing and figuring things out. Every day is different, and their abilities, thoughts, feelings and interests are fluid. I thought the guitar was gone forever and here it is again. My son was not ready then, but he is now. What you are seeing now in your child is not the final product. You can see glimpses of their future adult self, but the story is not yet told. Be patient, keep opportunities and options open and see what happens. As my old Uncle Erwin use to say, you need to "put it out on the stoop and see if the cat eats it." Things will often come back around if you are patient and wait. It is for this very reason that I kept my flannel shirts from college. I am now back in style! Better late than never I guess.

I hope you have a great weekend!

Andy

· · · · · ·

Hello Middle School Parents!

There were pieces everywhere! To me it looked like a total mess. Over 1000 pieces, marginally organized on a green folding table in our living room. That table is not normally there. It belongs folded up in the basement. There were two extra chairs in the living room as well. Those belong in the basement too. The clutter makes me shake a bit and doesn't everyone have a crazy uncle living in their basement? Where was he going to eat his dinner? And there they were. My wife and daughter had the nerve to sit in those chairs and work on the puzzle. The dish washer was clean and needed to be emptied (with more than the normal amount of upside down bowls with clean dirty water in them), The dogs needed to be fed (getting shocked by the fence builds up their appetite), the inlayed mahogany recycling bins needed to be put away and the new hot water heater needed to be polished and waxed. Looks like I am the beast of burden who is going to pull the "keep the family afloat" wagon today. Seriously? You two are going to take an hour and do a puzzle in the middle of the week? I didn't say this out loud, but I thought it, and they knew it.

The next day at school, there was a puzzle on the counter in the library. It was a puzzle of a bunch of kittens playing with yarn. Cats and puzzles. Nice. I walked by and started working on it with a student while I tried to convince him to go to math class. One of the principals came over and put in a piece, completing the nose of an almond colored British Shorthair. He explained that his mom buys a new puzzle each summer and leaves it out for anyone to work on. Anyone with some time to spare. The summer is a great time to have time. Waiting for the hower after being on the beach? Work on the puzzle. Not our turn to make lunch? Work on the puzzle. Slow, slow, low. This puzzle tradition helped me to solve my own uzzle. I was the one who was missing it. The buzz and o-go-go routine of life had shaded the slow down and enoy the moment side of my brain. Shouldn't we make having time a priority and not just in the summer? The end f the school year is so full of activities and obligations hat I was neglecting to slow down and see the kittens. I now working on a puzzle with my daughter is more important than any of these things that fill up a daily schedle and yet I was unable to see this. What to do?? Below re a few reminders to help us all slow down:

- Turn off all technology. I know technology is reported to make our lives richer and better, but I think for many it has had the opposite effect. Too often the phones are something that many people lack the discipline and willpower to regulate properly, creating a time vortex that is hard to get out of. When each family member is on their screen, it creates a segmented and isolated atmosphere. Be a role model and turn it off!
- Eat dinner together. Cook dinner together. Prioritize it. Make it happen. 40 minutes a day together can make a big difference in communication and strengthening family bonds.
- Do things together as a family. Go white water rafting, take a bike ride, or make cookies in the shape of cats.
- Schedule events with some time in between them. Running from one thing to the next causes stress. Time to breath in between can help.
- Don't buy so much stuff! The more things you have, the more things you have that need to be repaired,

maintained and dealt with. (The exception to this rule are boats, fishing equipment and high-quality power tools.)

- Leave the house. It can be hard to break away from the chores and technology. Go outside! (Try playing "find the pile" in the yard. You need two "spotters," and one "collector." Other necessary equipment is a pooper scooper and disposable shoes. Great game for birthday parties too.)

- Have everyone help! When a job needs to be done around the house, have everyone pitch in.

- Live in the "here and now." Enjoy the moment. Find the value of the current situation and the reason to be happy that are all around us.

I realize we have spoken about many of these ideas before, but at this time of year a reminder can't hurt! Have a great weekend!

Andy

• • • • • •

Hello Middle School Parents!

I vividly remember the biggest miscommunication mistake I ever made. My son was two weeks old, it was 2:30 in the morning and he was crying from his room down the hallway. Without thinking, and in a tired daze, I gently nudged my wife with my foot (some accounts use the word "kick," but I refute that) accompanied by the words, "honey, the baby is up..." Upon realizing what I had done, in a cold sweat, I prepared for the maternal/marital storm to hit, and it did…as time passed, I eventually got comfortable sleeping in the recycling bins. Empty gallon milk jugs make surprisingly decent pillows.

Communicating with your middle school child can be just as perilous! Below are a few ideas that might help to keep the lines of communication clear and open with your child and minimize unnecessary misunderstandings and arguments:

- Ask your child how their school day went and do so when you have time to listen. Ask questions that can't be answered with a simple yes or no. I will often ask my kids, "tell me something funny that happened in school today." Answer your own question as well, making it a two-way conversation. If nothing funny happened at your job, consider purchasing my newest book, "101 Practical Jokes in the Work Place that Won't Get you Fired."
- Be a good listener and really pay attention. Repeat back the most salient points of what your child is saying so they know you are with them. This can be very difficult especially when you are having trouble following what they are saying or start to lose focus. This week a student told me, "my dad always listens to me and I even bore myself sometimes!" True story.
- Point out their body language and the message it sends to you. This can be done in a calm, conversational way. "Sally, when you made an L with your hand on your forehead and mouthed the word 'loser' to your mother, she interpreted that as disrespectful." This can help increase their self-awareness and improve their communication skills.

- Write it down. When you have rules that need to be followed or an agreement has been reached, write it down and post it where you can all see it. This helps avoid misunderstandings about what was agreed upon. "Johnny, please refer to the signed rules on the refrigerator. It clearly states that when you bungie cord your younger brother to the oak tree we take your phone for two weeks."
- Avoid sitting your kids down and saying "OK, let's talk about your feelings now." That is just weird and a total turn off. Let the conversation happen naturally while doing something you both enjoy. Baking cookies, shooting baskets, fishing etc. Kids are more likely to talk when active and engaged in a shared activity.
- The kids, even at an early age, know when you are not paying attention and they know when you are slinging the BS. Yesterday, I was trying to listen to the news in the car while my daughter was explaining why it would be fun to go to school with Sponge Bob. After I absently said "that's cool" two times, she said, "you are not even listening are you?" I turned off the radio and asked her to start again. Be genuine and interested in your interactions with your children and they will continue to communicate with you.

(Now you know why my recycling bins are so important to me!)

I hope you have a great weekend!

Andy

• • • • • •

136

Hello Middle School Parents!

Believe it or not, we are getting ready to start the course selection process for high school. You just got a little nervous, didn't you? The number of courses offered can be staggering. It is akin to a huge academic buffet. You and your child have a warm clean plate and you are getting ready to awkwardly bend down past the sneeze guard and start piling on heaps of AP, Honors and Accelerated classes...yum. The trick is not to overeat, as you might make yourself and your kid sick. I also have insider knowledge and heard you have been talking to your friend who has been very generous with providing suggestions and advice regarding course selection. She is a self-proclaimed expert on high school, having seen High School Musical and Fast Times at Ridgemont High...

Below are a few things I would like you to think about:

- Every child is different. What is right for one student may not be right for another. Just because your older child, neighbor or friend's kid was in AP Biology does not necessarily mean your other child should be.

- Have reasonable expectations for your child. Just because you went to an Ivy League school does mean your kid will. (Your spouse definitely watered down the genes but that is a different story.)

- If being happy and enjoying high school is on your list of objectives, finding a balance between academics and everything else that is important to your child is critical. Could they take all the most challenging classes offered? Maybe. Would your kids be a stressed-out mess with little time for family, friends or extracurricular activities? Probably.

- When it comes to selecting classes, stay focused on pursuing challenges in areas of genuine interest and having new and exciting experiences.
- Don't focus on what you think colleges would want to see, instead think about what would provide your child with an amazing and memorable 4 years of high school.
- I guess what I am saying is don't overdo it with all this stuff. If you listen to the teachers, your child, and your gut instincts about what is right, everything will work out for the best.

I hope you have a great weekend!

Andy

· · · · · ·

Choosing classes: part 2

Hello Middle School Parents!

As part 2 of my new series, "don't overdo it," I will share with you a brief and true conversation I had with a student while working at the high school. Sally (10th grade) came into my office in tears. She told me she was under a lot of pressure because she wanted to attend Harvard. I inquired about her desire to attend this prestigious school. Perhaps she was driven to find a cure for a disease, make a lot of money or maybe to study a certain subject at the highest level possible. When I asked her this "why do you want to go to Harvard" question, she looked at me like I was crazy. I get this look often (especially at home) so I am typically aware when people think I have lost my mind. Sally paused for a while thinking about the questions I had posed to her. Eventually she responded. "Mr.

Mullen, I want to attend Harvard because it is the best."
She started crying again.

- Many parent's are geared toward "the best." I don't care which "the best" you or your kid are going for; college, car, house, travel team etc. With those expectations and standards, you are at risk for unhealthy levels of stress. Maybe going for "the best I can attain while still being happy" is a better way to think about it. (Exceptions to this rule are: power tools, boat engines and urologists. Get the best you can, at all costs.)
- Stress is the number one problem for high school kids (unofficial statistic, but my own observations from working in the high school for 4 years.)
- Course selection is an excellent opportunity to role model reasonable behavior and contribute to an environment of calm and logical thinking. Involvement, concern, discussion, and consideration are all good things and by most accounts can be implemented in a productive way.
- Don't drink the cool-aid. It is hard not to get wrapped up in the crazy town of high performance and keeping up with everyone. Do your own thing. Use common sense and hold the line on what is important to you and your family.
- Whatever you do, don't let your kid overeat at the academic buffet! Remind your child to put down their academic fork, take a deep breath and have fun... or you will have a lot of cleaning up to do!

hope you have a great weekend!

Andy

• • • • • •

Hello Middle School Parents!

It can sneak up on you, like a panther in the jungle, a highly trained ninja warrior or even old age. If not kept in check, it can slowly eat away at your entire existence and undermine every goal and dream of happiness you ever had. What am I talking about? No, it's not marriage, taxes or your muffin top. The topic this week is stress!

The amazing ability of the human body to prepare you for "fight or flight" has helped our species survive, and in small doses can help us perform at our highest level. If, however, stress persists for a long period of time it can have devastating effects on our health. Stress is often seen as an inevitable part of adolescence, and because of this we are often slow to intervene to reduce the stress in our kids. We live in a high stress society and our kids attend competitive schools. High stress coupled with ineffective coping strategies are ingrained in our culture. Adolescents often cite school as the most common source of stress. Below are some warning signs you can look for in your child (and in some cases yourself), as well as some suggestions for how to take control and manage everyday stress. I call it "taming the tiger" to stay with the large cat theme already established...

Signs of stress in adolescents:
- Withdrawing from friendships and activities they usually enjoy.
- Excessive crying
- Refusing to go to school
- Aggressive behavior

- Severe decrease in school grades
- Feeling sick often
- Not eating or loss of appetite
- Being more tired than usual even though they are getting plenty of sleep
- Difficulty focusing
- Difficulty remembering things
- Being cranky or moody
- Feeling sad, worthless or hopeless

Possible sources of stress:
- School demands
- Changes in their bodies
- Problems with friends
- Divorce or separation of parents
- Chronic illness or severe problems in the family
- Death of a loved one
- Taking on too many activities or having expectations that are too high
- Family financial problems

What you can do to help your child:
- Listen to your child and watch for signs they are overwhelmed.
- Learn and model healthy stress management strategies. Exercise, meditation, yoga etc.
- Have your child speak to their counselor about figuring out which ways will help them to reduce and manage their stress.

I hope you have a great weekend!

Andy

• • • • • •

Hello Middle School Parents!

Leather. High quality dark green leather lavishly hugging a hard wood frame. This was a beautiful piece of furniture to last a lifetime. Permanent. Perhaps the last oversized chair we would ever buy. We were optimistically young with a shallow sense of time. Four dogs, three kids and 20 years later, our leather flagship was tired and worn like a stone in a slow-moving brook. Our perception was skewed, clouded by history and proximity. We were blinded, unable to see the effects of time and use. "The chair in the den is not looking so good" my oldest son pointed out. My wife and I paused, surprised, looking at it together. Were those scratches from our first dog, a 120-pound Newfoundland, or years of kids wrestling on it? Where did the tear in the ottoman come from? I remember! My middle son sat on it with a pencil in his back pocket years ago. Maybe this chair was not going to last forever. Did anything?

The mail came this week and in it was a letter addressed to my oldest son. The penmanship familiar but out of context. Inside it revealed an old letter he had written to his 12th grade self. Dreams, goals and aspirations poured out, some realized others forgotten. His 8th grade English teacher, each year, has her students write letters to themselves and lovingly mails them home four years later. Amazing. Where had the time gone? How could my son be graduating from high school? The chair is new, we just bought that. My son. He is a baby, wrapped up like a burrito in my arms, as I slowly dance with him at a colicky 2 a.m., praying he falls asleep. The days go slow and the years go fast.

142

I am reminded of this more and more as my kids grow. Take the time, cherish the moment and be present with your family. You only get one go at being a mom or a dad. You, and everything that goes with you will still be there when they leave. You will still have time to focus on you. The 18-year window with each of your children will close before you realize it. The other day my 6th grade daughter was laughing with my 12th grade son in the kitchen. I put down my dish towel, leaned back on the counter and soaked it all it. Leather chairs, a full nest and a brook that never stops flowing...

I hope you have a wonderful weekend enjoying your family!

Andy

June

· · · · · ·

Hello Middle School Parents!

Did you know that the annual Williamsburg trip is coming up next week? Are you starting to get nervous? Maybe just a little? For many children, this is the first time away from the nest without parental supervision. It is very normal to wonder how your child will act and if they will be OK without you. How will they ever function without their cell phone? Will they purchase the 20-pound Gummy Bear in the gift store? What about the risk of overeating cotton candy at Kings Dominion and barfing on the bus ride home? Will they roll their eyes at their chaperone and call them "annoying" like they do to you? Perhaps this is a good time for us to talk about "letting go" as parents and allowing our kids to assert some independence. Below are a few things to think about:

- Believe in yourself! You have done your best to raise your child. Have faith that your child has the necessary manners and maturity.
- Are you polite and nice? If so, your child is probably polite and nice as well. (The whole apple/tree thing.)
- Developmentally, your child craves and needs some independence.
- Encourage some risk taking. The good kind. Run for class president, try out for the team, learn a new instrument. They need to do the stuff that makes them get a pit in their stomach. We get the same excitement and rush from a "good risk" (making a speech) as a "bad" one (stealing car, driving to Vegas and gambling away college money.)
- Take a back seat and let your kid solve their own problems, make some choices and manage the consequences, negative and positive. This is how they learn.
- Start making more jokes. Your kids are older and have the ability to understand your humor. When you have to be stern, make rules or correct them, adding a pinch of humor can help them listen to you and keep the conversation pleasant.
- Acknowledge your child's maturity and their ability to think for themselves.
- To quote my old Vice Principal, Ed Kershner, "Middle school is a bunch of hormones and sneakers." The boy/ girl stuff is something you will have to deal with at some point. How much independence do you give? A safe rule many parents use is to only allow group activities.
- Talk with your spouse or other trusted adult and periodically discuss some new privileges or rights you think your child might be ready for.

- Doing too much for your kid can result in a self-centered child with very little problem-solving skills. Do less for them!

Just can't do it? If "letting them go" and reducing the amount you protect and coddle your child is something you need help with, the summer camp below might be for you!

Have you heard of a new summer opportunity called *Camp Safety Last?* This is a new camp (that I am running), taught by mostly competent instructors, in which your children will learn about many things in life that you have been afraid to teach them! Some of the hands on instructional units may include but are not limited to:

- The Art of Chain Sawing While Tired
- Small Animal Game Hunting in the Suburbs
- Driving Boats Fast Can Be Fun
- How to Burn Just About Anything
- Throwing Stars Are Not Just for Ninjas
- Measure Once, Cut Twice. Advanced Power Tool Usage for Beginners
- 101 Creative Uses for Leftover Fireworks

I hope you have a great weekend!

Andy

• • • • • •

When the kids are away

Hello Middle School Parents!

Do you notice anything different around the house? Does something seem amiss? Perhaps there is a mild sense of calm, the source of which is eluding you. I must remind you that your 7th grader is not home! What are you supposed to do? You need to have a plan of action to take full advantage of this unprecedented, uncommon and unbelievable opportunity! Here are a few ideas for your consideration while the kids are away:

- Get some mild revenge. You have been dealing with their middle school antics for three years now, it is time they paid the piper. Purchase a "room for rent" sign and prominently place it in the front yard. Pay the weird 30-year-old who lives in his mother's basement to take a nap in your child's room, only to be discovered by your child upon their return from Williamsburg.
- Purchase 40 pounds of unsliced, whole salami and hang them from the ceiling of your kid's room. When they return, tell them you have a new hobby of meat preservation and from a humidity and temperature perspective, their room is the best option.
- Turn their room into the hot yoga studio you have always wanted.
- Watch Scarface, Silence of the Lambs and other horrifyingly awesome movies you have not been able to watch for the past 12 years.
- Curse like crazy to get it out of your system.
- Pick up the charged iPad that is exactly where you left it the night before and enjoy a cup of coffee in the morning while reading the weird stuff your kid's counselor sends you.
- Clean the recycling bins, together, as a couple...

I hope you have a great next few days and a wonderful weekend!

Andy

• • • • • •

Hello Middle School Parents!

Graduations, presentations, parties, games, events, wow! The list of obligations all seem to collect and get jammed into the end of the school year. It is like a water slide when the one kid stops himself and the whole tube gets clogged. It can feel like every day and night you are running from one thing to another and finding time to slow down is getting harder and harder. We have been so busy at my house I even had to decline a coveted invitation to brunch with my mother-in-law. Oh, the pain. With this crazy pace can come stress, frustration, fatigue and an overall sense of not being organized. These, coincidentally, are the main factors that can contribute to us losing our temper with our kids. Even the best parents have stories of losing control during times of stress and acting in ways we would not normally act. To prevent yourself from "dumping the rice" (a reference from the show Survivor) and completely losing your ****, here are few thoughts that might help:

- Try to figure out what angers you the most. Talking back, lying, eye-rolling, complaining? What are your triggers for losing your temper? If you can identify these triggers, you may be able to implement some of the strategies below before you chase your kid around the house hurling obscenities at that little ungrateful, rude, disrespectful…sorry, I was starting to get angry…
- Come up with a plan ahead of time for dealing with those situations that drive you crazy. If you know

lying sends you off the deep end, have a set consequence and way of dealing with it in place that you can implement as needed. This can help you avoid saying crazy things like "I will never feed you dinner ever again!" or perhaps, "I am going to trade you in at the township building for a nice kid!"

- Take a deep breath. Breathing is so underrated. Remind yourself to breath before you speak or act. A student once said to me, "Mr. Mullen, I just wish there was a speed bump between my brain and my mouth." Install your own speed bump and think before you act.

- Walk away. Far away. Remove yourself from the situation so you can't see or hear that little rat weasel kid of yours. (Sorry, angry again.) Calm down then decide what to do.

- Imagine that the child in front of you is not yours. How would you react? It is so much easier to stay calm and act appropriately when it is not your kid. Have you ever seen a child behaving terribly at a restaurant or out in public and you smile and feel some empathy for the parents? You don't get angry because it is not your kid.

- When talking with your child, speak softly and slowly. This can help deescalate a situation.

- Don't take their behavior personally. Their behavior is not a reflection of you or your parenting skills. Remember, they are testing the waters. This is all part of growing up and the challenge of being a parent. Look at the situation analytically not emotionally.

- What calms you down? What are your healthy go to things that help you relax? Yoga, running, talking, meditating? Stop and do these things when you start to sense your triggers are activated.

- To help avoid the stress before it starts, keep a family calendar that everyone can see. Also, making a few dinners on Sunday for the following week can help reduce the crazy factor.
- If all else fails look into the Kid Replacement Program (KRP): This program is for parents who wish to trade in their child for one that does their homework, cleans their room and is kind and considerate towards their siblings and parents all of the time. These children are specially designed to have an aversion to eye rolling. They love doing household chores including, but not limited to, cleaning out recycling bins, taking out the trash, picking up after the dog and scrubbing the soap scum from showers. Please call me if you are ready to upgrade!

I hope you have a great weekend!

Andy

• • • • • •

Dads and daughters

Hello Middle School Parents!

Dads can be awesome! Just this week I heard a couple of stories that reminded me how important the role of a father can be in the life of his adolescent daughter. The one story was simply a dad inviting his daughter to watch television with him. The other was a calm and genuine response when his daughter shared her feelings. In both instances, the girls came in to tell me how important and meaningful these interactions with their fathers were. It is all of the little things that add up to a healthy and trusting father/daughter relationship! Let's take a closer look:

I must mention that there are many families for various reasons, without a traditional "father." This role, however, can be assumed, very successfully, by other caring and loving people in the life of a child.]

- It is so easy to shy away from a hormonal, standoffish daughter. It is now that they need you the most! Work to build a trusting relationship so that your daughter feels comfortable talking to you about what is going on in her life. Take the time to listen to her thoughts. Let her do the talking. Don't give up if she pushes you away.
- When she does talk to you, resist the urge to go right into a lecture. Listen and talk to her about your concerns when the time is right. When she tells you she is madly in love and will be running away to Wynnewood or somewhere else really far away, stay calm and let her finish.
- Provide your daughter with affection and support. They still need hugs and will for the rest of their lives!
- Battle low self-esteem. Give your daughter verbal encouragement and focus on what she is doing right. Tell her you love her, you are proud of her and that she is strong and smart and pretty!
- Take an active interest in her hobbies. You may not enjoy basketball but get out there and shoot the rock if your daughter enjoys it! (I draw the line at scrapbooking, but everything else is a go.)
- Be alert and sensitive to her feelings. Has she been crying, or does it look like she had a hard day? Take the time to notice and ask her about it.

- Go to her events. I know you are busy, but get to her game, play, concert, recital, match, whatever. It makes a difference and she will remember
- Tell her about your day and share your interests with her. Your wife is not interested, but your daughter might be! Don't assume she won't be interested in splitting firewood, watching the Eagles game, burning things, adjusting the laser site on your miter saw, or any other manly activities you engage in. Let her decide, you might be surprised.
- Don't "turn off" your emotional side just because you think your wife handles that.
- Be the kind of man you want your daughter to marry. You are her model for what men are and should be. Act with honesty and integrity.
- For the dads that have not had a great deal of interaction with their girls, now is a good time to start. It is not too late!

I hope you have a wonderful weekend!

Andy

• • • • • •

Adolescent bacon

Hello Middle School Parents!

I decided to cook bacon today. It was raining, chilly and Friday. A perfect day for slow cooking a pound of salted, cured, pork belly. The aroma gently prodded my children out of bed before their caustic sounding alarm clocks. Nice. As I stood vigil over the large cast iron skillet at 5:00 a.m., diligently tending the little strips of heaven, I started to think about how similar and dissimilar bacon is to middle school students...no I am not on medication...yet:

- Bacon smells good, middle schoolers do not.
- Everyone loves bacon. Not the case for adolescents.
- Bacon is predictable and consistent. Middle schoolers not so much.
- Kids can be greasy. Bacon can be too. Both can be blotted with paper towels.
- Bacon is good on everything. Middle schoolers are best by themselves.
- Bacon is easy to cook and take care of. Kids are not!
- Bacon can sizzle and spit. Adolescents can spit too.
- In moderation, both can be amazing, but overexposure can be deleterious to one's health.

I hope you have a wonderful weekend filled with breakfast meats!

Andy

• • • • • •

The end is near

Hello Middle School Parents!

The fog can be very thick. From your vantage point, things are blurry, and you don't know where you are headed. There could be amazing things all around you which pass unnoticed. The ever-present fear of the unknown can keep you on edge, waiting for the worst. Anxiety rules and frustration permeates your being. It may seem like this state of unrest and turmoil has been going on forever (4 years to be exact). When will this all end?

Well, the 8th grade promotion is next week, so that might be a start!

Middle school has the power to make even the best kid seem like an overwhelmingly gigantic jerk (OGJ) and rather unpleasant to parent. Why is this so? There are many reasons, but the short answer is confusion and insecurity. The kids are confused about who they are, and they lack confidence. In adolescence, there is an ever-present low level of fear and uncertainty. Have you ever noticed how small dogs bark and bite more often than bigger dogs? (I don't mean to compare your child to a dog again, but I just can't stop.) I think it is because they are afraid, nervous and lack confidence. I guess what I am saying is your kid is a small, yappy, insecure dog child. While some children do bite, their insecurities typically manifest themselves in how poorly they treat each other and their parents. What does the future hold? Will you forever be stuck in this foggy world of adolescent chaos?

I have some incredible news for you! You are on the tail end (dog pun) of this stage. The kids are maturing each day, looking and acting more like high school kids. What might the end product look like? What do you have to look forward to? When the fog clears, and the sun is shining, you will have an unobstructed view of the fruits of your labors as parents. I have been talking with my former students who are now senior interns here at the middle school. Without fail, they are mature, confident, and self-assured. These impressive young adults are ready for life. They too were once annoying, yappy, unsettled middle schoolers, diligently acting like OGJs to their parents and peers. Good weather with high visibility is in your parental forecast! I have foreseen it to be so!!

154

I hope you have a great weekend,

Andy

* * * * * *

Hello Middle School Parents!

The summer is here! What are you going to do? It is crazy how the years fly by. Having the summers to spend with your middle school kids is such a gift (really, it is) and the time can slip by so quickly. Take full advantage of this opportunity and make some amazing memories. Here are a few ideas for you and your family to think about:

- Totally unplug. If you go on vacation, you and your kids should turn off and put away the cell phones. This is liberating and allows you all to reset and get back to basics. Things like talking to each other, looking around instead of down and being present in the here and now are good things.
- Go back to the 1970's! I vividly remember being outside all day, working on my burn, playing Wiffle Ball (you still can't hit my knuckle ball), swimming and having completely unstructured time to be a kid. Allow your kids this same opportunity and embrace it! Play some Lynyrd Skynyrd, put on some tight OP shorts, relax and play with your kids. Having nothing planned is awesome. Unstructured time also allows your kids to use their imagination.
- Use all of the vacation/personal time you can. The kids are only young once. When possible, take more than a few days off so you can get into a relaxed vacation tempo. I think in the travel business

155

they call this the rhythm method, but I may be wrong on that.

- The school year is crazy busy with homework, sports, etc. Perhaps your kids have not had time to really help with the daily chores around the house. Consider creating new responsibilities for the kids during the summer months. Cooking lunch, folding the laundry, whatever helps your home run, they can contribute. For example, at Camp Safety Last, the kids are learning how to prune trees close to power lines. When a minimal level of competency is reached this could be on their weekly chore list.

- Go Paintballing! The kids might be ready for this now. I recommend finding the people with annual memberships, wearing camouflage, toting their own high-end equipment, and challenge them to a game. Pain can be good for the kids.

- When it is hot and humid, and you need time inside, have the kids watch the original Karate Kid. When it cools down, they can wax your car.

- Do something new that is outside of your comfort zone. Try a new restaurant, go camping, visit a town you have always wanted to see. Doing something new can be energizing and breaking the routine can be refreshing. (If you go camping, you may want to sprinkle hot dogs around the tent perimeter to allow the kids to see wildlife really close up. Let me know how that goes.)

- What did you love to do before you had kids? Maybe the kids are ready to learn and participate in those activities. Long bike rides, fly fishing, golfing, knitting, wild boar hunting. If you loved it, maybe your kids will too.

- Having amazing family time does not mean spending a ton of money. It means sharing real time together, laughing and having fun.
- Too much family time? Need some time without the kids? Play and sing along with the song "Wannabe" from the Spice Girls and your kids will leave you alone. Guaranteed to work. Tried it last night and it cleared the room.

Editor's Note: (Full disclosure) I am doing a total 180 on the recycling bin cleaning thing. Are you licking the recycling bins or eating your beef stew out of them? No!! Please call me to discuss if you are.) I am no longer cleaning my recycling bins. Like ever! You do what you want but I am embracing the dirt and filth and leveraging the found time to play professional Wiffle Ball!

I hope you have a wonderful summer!

Andy

Conclusion

· · · · · ·

Hello Middle School Parents!

I think this is it! Year-end activities are upon us, the kids are tired of each other, tired of school and ready to move on. I imagine you might be ready for middle school to be over as well. Middle school is one of those unavoidable life events that we try to make as pleasant as possible. I guess it is akin to having a comfortable chair to get a root canal in or perhaps a very nice, fresh barf bag during a turbulent plane ride. Either way, I hope your journey as parents of a middle schooler was one you will fondly (too strong a word perhaps?) remember.

The weekly messages have allowed me to reflect on my own daily life and to take notice of the embedded messages and lessons that are all around me. My efforts to seek out the humor in the mundane and to draw connections in raising middle school aged children has been an enlightening and entertaining exercise. Lastly, the messages have held me accountable for my observations as both a parent and counselor and for this I am grateful.

Thank you for reading *Middle Schooled*. I hope it allowed you to learn and laugh while on this middle school adventure. I figured laughing was better than crying, that was the idea anyway!

Andy

Acknowledgements

· · · · · ·

Thank you to my wife, Toni, for spending countless hours reading and editing this book with me. She told me honestly when what I was writing was not funny, offensive and eventually right on target. I wrote about families working together as a team and Toni is without question our team captain! I love you!

So much of this book is based on experiences I have had as a parent with my own children. Thank you, Drew, Jake and Maggie for seriously being the best. Of course, I love you all. The truth is that I actually like each of you, a lot, even when you were/are in middle school! Our time spent together as a family is truly the greatest gift of my life.

Without the encouragement from the parents of my students over the years, this book would never have been written. Thank you for your positive feedback on the weekly e-mails I send out and for so many of you suggesting I write a book! Thank you for giving me the confidence to make this happen!

Thank you to Scott Reidenbach for your legal- council and encouragement!

Thank you to my wonderful Canadian friend Glennda Olivier for your precise edits and suggestions for helping to make *Middle Schooled* as universally friendly as possible!

Steve and Jenny McSherry. Two of the most intelligent and considerate people I know. Thank you both for reading *Middle Schooled* and for your genuine interest and thoughtful feedback   Most importantly, thank you for being such good friends!

Thank you to my talented and grounded friend Emelie Collet for your unique and thoughtful perspective.

Thank you to Keri Phillips for your early proofing of *Middle Schooled*. It was quite a grammatical mess at that time!!

Lastly, I would like to thank every middle school student there is and ever was. Without your insecurities, quirkiness and unique behaviors, I would have had nothing to write about!

Made in the USA
Monee, IL
15 September 2020